Escape from the Grip

£2·00

④

Escape from the Grip

by

JUDY WURMBRAND

HODDER AND STOUGHTON
LONDON SYDNEY AUCKLAND TORONTO

ISBN 0 340 228016

First published 1979. Second impression 1979

*Photoset and printed in Great Britain for
Hodder and Stoughton Limited,
Mill Road, Dunton Green, Sevenoaks, Kent
by Lowe and Brydone Printers Limited,
Thetford, Norfolk*

I dedicate this book
to the very best of parents I was privileged to have:
JENNY and HERMAN, who gave me life and taught me survival,
and MILLY and MEIR LEVY, who guided me spiritually.
With deep respect, love and gratitude,

JUDY

Contents

Chapter Five

Chapter Six

Chapter Seven

Chapter Eight

Chapter Nine

PROLOGUE

August, 1942, near the border between Ukraine and Romania.

Running through the dark forest, Herman stumbled and fell again. Once more he picked himself up and hurried on. The border, he had to get to the border, to the river Bug. Romania was there, on the other side, and Romania meant freedom. Now that his bare feet were bleeding, he was afraid the German shepherd dogs would scent him, so he pressed on.

A shout came suddenly behind him.

'Stoi!'

Herman stopped. 'That is the end,' he thought, and remained motionless for another few seconds, waiting for the voice to approach. Herman could now see an old, bearded Ukrainian guard, holding a gun.

'What are you doing here, young man, at this hour of the night?' asked the Ukrainian.

'What am I doing? Trying to find my way home, of course,' Herman answered in broken Ukrainian.

'Home? You don't sound like a Ukrainian, young man.'

'Well, no . . . I'm not . . .'

'Are you running away? . . .' Herman nodded, ' . . . From the German concentration camp of Yarishev? Don't you know the Germans are all over the place? They'll catch you in no time.'

'Yes, I know. But what do I have to lose? My name was on the death list this morning.'

The guard sighed. 'Yes, what do we all have to lose? My own son, you know, he was taken to the front last year. I have not heard from him since. Who knows where he is now? Maybe he's running too . . .'

The old man's voice became milder, his arm on the shotgun relaxed.

'All right, young man. Where do you want to go?'

'To Mogilev. I was told I would find people there who could shelter me.'

'Mogilev, hmm . . . Go straight ahead, for about a mile, till you get to the river Bug. Follow the river for another mile till you come to a bridge. Be sure to cross it, the Romanian zone is on the other side. If you meet people, don't talk to anyone, just walk on. Usually there is only one soldier watching that point. Don't attract his attention. He wouldn't be very helpful to a fugitive Jew.'

'Thank you for your kindness, grandpa. God bless you.'

'God bless you and go with you, my child, and don't say a word about me if you are caught. They would shoot me too. Not that I'd mind, but I may be useful again to some other lads like you.'

'Of course, grandpa, I understand. God be with you.'

What incredible luck! Herman hurried on. Get to the river, to the bridge. 'If only I could sit down for a while . . . but those dogs are after me . . .'

Still walking, he fetched a piece of corn-meal bread out of his light bundle and took a few bites. How good it tasted! Ten hours he had been running, and it wasn't over yet. Who knew when it would end, and how?

A faint path gleamed between the tree-trunks. How long that mile seemed. Trudging on wearily, Herman recalled his childhood days, when the way to school also seemed endless to his little legs. He felt so tired when he finally got to school. He felt even more tired now, but school or river were nowhere in sight.

Suddenly he froze. Under the cover of the trees, a German soldier was standing, twenty feet away, pointing his gun at him.

'Again,' Herman thought, fighting down his first impulse to run: that would have been fatal. 'Why be afraid?' insisted a sharp inner voice. 'That German soldier won't know any Ukrainian; besides, I am dressed like a Ukrainian peasant. I'll pass as Ukrainian, he won't know the difference. I'll sit down and act as though I did not see him.'

Herman sat on the ground as nonchalantly as he could, took out his cigarette papers and tobacco, and rolled a cigarette, controlling each movement and trying to look relaxed.

With a fierce look in his eyes, the German soldier in his

well-polished boots was approaching steadily, gun at the ready.

'Hey, swine, what are you doing here?' he barked in German.

Herman looked at the soldier, still rolling the cigarette, and motioned ahead of him. Cold sweat was trickling down his spine. For a second he wished the soldier would shoot him right there and get it over. 'So what if I am only 20 years old? I'm sick of this life, this constant fear' he thought.

'Where are you going? the soldier shouted.

'Home, home' answered Herman in Ukrainian, pointing towards the river and Romania.

The soldier pointed to his bundle. 'Open!'

Herman opened it. There was some corn-meal and milk left. The soldier hesitated. Beside the fact that he was walking on border territory, Herman looked innocent. The soldier made a gesture of disgust. 'Move on and don't come back.'

Herman picked up his bundle and started away, afraid at each step that the German might shoot him in the back. After a few endless minutes, reckoning he was safely out of shooting range, Herman looked back and saw the soldier resting under a tree.

'Another miracle!' he thought. 'Thank you Lord, THANK YOU!'

Scrambling quickly downhill he soon reached the Bug. Instead of following the bank until he found a bridge, he plunged straight in, dogs still in mind. The cold water bit into his scratched and weary body, and waves of hunger, fright and exhaustion pulled at him. The current lapped and curled against his chest. Only the indescribable prospect of survival gave him enough strength to claw through to the reeds of the opposite bank, where he slumped, drained.

When he returned to full consciousness the sky was already lightening. Soaked and shivering he clambered up the bank and stumbled on; there was a metalled road, foolish to follow, but he was past caring. One step followed another.

Round a bend in the road a bar across the way gleamed in the early light. He had reached the Romanian frontier. As he paused and looked, something attracted his eye in the squat guardhouse: he peered forward, and then smiled grimly. The border guard was busy with a girl, and preferred to ignore him. Now he was in Romania! A warm feeling enveloped him. He was back in his country!

On the road peasants on foot and in carts formed a long stream all moving slowly in one direction: to the market in Mogilev. Among them Herman noticed a woman carrying a heavy load of potatoes. Instinctively he went to relieve her. The woman was glad of the help and it turned out to be a wonderful decoy for Herman. German soldiers were passing on the road, looking for men trying to escape, such as him.

Herman walked with the woman for a couple of miles. But the potatoes got heavier and heavier, his bare feet more and more painful until he just could not walk any more. He had to rest. He lay down under a bush off the road and fell asleep immediately. Nothing could disturb him – the noise of passing carts, mooing animals, peasants shouting to each other. He just slept. Later when he woke up, refreshed, he mixed again with a group of peasants walking to Mogilev. They were taking a round-about way in order to avoid a special tax upon entering the town. This was perfect for Herman who wanted to avoid the soldiers at the tax point, since they were also checking passes.

Once in Mogilev, he looked for the Jewish ghetto, knocked at the first door he came upon and collapsed in the doorway. The people took him in, gave him some water and put him on a bed where he slept for a solid twenty-four hours.

January 1943

All surviving Jews in North-Eastern Romania were crowded into the ghetto of Yeruga, near Mogilev. Each day they worked eighteen hours, felling and loading timber for the Romanian Army. Dull axes were their most sophisticated tool, and their one hot meal a day consisted of ground corn cobs boiled in salt water.

Beatings were frequent, but the Nazi-supporting Romanians did not kill Jews so consistently as the Nazis themselves. For that privilege one had to be grateful in those dark years, and Herman was duly grateful. Somewhere his name was still on a list to be shot.

A typhoid epidemic broke out in the crowded and insanitary ghetto. People were dying right and left, and he soon developed its terrible symptoms. Dragged to the foul room that made shift as a hospital ward, he lay for several days on the floor, delirious or unconscious. At his side another young man and his mother endured the same agony, only they had a relative who came each day to care for them, a young and pretty redhead. In a lucid moment he watched as she fed them warm soup. How he wished that one of his four sisters, or his mother, could be there to care for him. But where were his sisters and mother?

The young woman, called Jenny, befriended him, even though she was already caring for her sick mother and brother. This was very unusual, for in such conditions friendship was a scarce commodity: one of the vilest outcomes of concentration camp existence was that most people, weary beyond description with the struggle for food and clothing, abandoned their nearest and dearest, shedding responsibility rather than acquiring it, much less fell in love. But Herman and Jenny did.

What Jenny liked about Herman was his inextinguishable optimism, his firm determination to live through this horror and one day, somehow, get to America.

Those were my parents-to-be, who against all logic were engaged and swiftly married in that dreadful place, the guests feasting on a few crusts of dry black bread.

Perhaps in an unconscious defiance of their harsh life, Jenny soon became pregnant. She concealed it as long as she could – – the guards were mocking every pregnant woman –, but she could not help vomiting and fainting. This did not prevent the Romanian guards from beating her if she did not fulfil her work quota.

One day the prisoners were working in the shale pits, up to their knees in filthy water, digging big pieces of wet coal from the streaming surface. After a few hours, Jenny collapsed. Her mother and brother working by her dropped their tools to carry her to dry land. The guard rushed them back to work, cursing and wielding his whip.

'But she is too weak, she is pregnant, can't you see? Don't you have any pity?' protested her mother.

To curb her tongue, the guard lashed her across the back until she, too, fell, while Jenny's brother pleaded for them, promising to do their share of the work. When the guard stopped at last, his rage exhausted, the two women were unable to stand. It took them a week to recover. Their backs had turned black from the beating.

November 1943

In the unheated house, the stone walls shone like diamonds under the frost. Jenny was going into labour. The midwife of the village was sent for immediately. Twenty years ago she had been a nurse, and since there was no doctor, she was the only person who could help out in emergencies. She arrived, armed with a small bowl for the hot water and a pair of rusty scissors.

After four hours of terrible pains, Jenny gave birth to a baby girl, very pale and very, very skinny. The midwife swaddled her in pieces of linen cut from a sheet. Jenny lovingly embraced her and named her Frida, after her own father who had died of heart failure shortly after his arrival in the ghetto. As she lay exhausted on the sacking, Herman unexpectedly appeared in the doorway. He had slipped his work at the risk of a beating to spend a few precious moments with his baby. But the next day they noticed how pale the baby was. She had hepatitis. There was no medicine whatsoever on hand. The baby died that night. Those were sad days . . .

Beginning of 1944

The Soviets began to get the upper hand in Eastern Europe. As the Germans were retreating, the Romanians decided to change sides and ally with the Soviets, the obvious victors, against whom they had been fighting only hours before! The Russian 'liberation' meant little to the ghetto. All male Jews had now to toil just as hard for the Red Army as they had toiled for the Germans. Bombings had become a daily occurrence.

March 18, 1944

In celebration of their first wedding anniversary, Jenny prepared a feast: a dish of corn-meal sweetened with sugar beet. She carried the dish through the city, to the bridge Herman and other men were restoring. Just as they were about to eat, they heard an all too familiar droning . . . the daily German air-raid. They quickly scattered for cover, Jenny grabbing the precious dish of corn-meal. When the bombing stopped the ground was littered with corpses. More than two hundred people had been killed but Herman and Jenny were unharmed. They helped bury the dead, so it was only late that evening that they were finally ready to eat that corn-meal. But further blows shattered the brief moment of happy anticipation. A Russian officer and six of his soldiers came in and flatly announced that they were going to spend the night there. Though the one room shelter was hardly bigger than Herman and Jenny's bed, the soldiers promptly went to sleep on the bare floor and started snoring. The officer joined Herman and Jenny who were glad to share their 'home' and food with a representative of the 'liberating' Russian army. In that cosy atmosphere Herman started describing to the Russian officer the sufferings inflicted by the Germans. The Russian took a long look at him, then spat and turned away, muttering, 'Pity they didn't finish all of you.'

Soon all male Jews were seized to serve as 'pehota' (infantry) in the Russian front line. Physical fitness or military aptitude had nothing to do with it. Thousands were needed for the slaughter: it was a military necessity, and probably a convenient way of getting rid of more Jews. Women and even children were rounded up in this mindless conscription.

Taking advantage of the panic, Jenny and the four survivors in her family decided to flee to their home town of Chernowitz, and hide. But nothing could be done to save Herman. He was as good as dead, crammed in with hundreds of others, waiting for the train bound for their fatal destination.

Or so it seemed . . . because Herman never got aboard that train.

At the railway station a hundred and sixty women, old men and children, through bribing a Russian official, were waiting to be placed on another train, bound in the opposite direction. Convoys were leaving constantly. In the confusion one woman of this group, Clara Solomon, set out across the railway tracks with her four-year-old son in her arms, and stumbled and fell. A train struck her, throwing the boy clear. The only one who dared run to help her was Herman, but when he reached her she was already dead, her body grotesquely crumpled.

In the chaos and screaming that immediately erupted the boy clung to him, and Herman folded his arms around him. Seeing this, the group's leader elbowed his way through the mob of Russian soldiers and Jews, and offered Herman the life-giving chance of becoming 'Carl' Solomon through the exit-papers he held, and thus escaping the Red Army's butchery. Naturally, he was glad to accept. Against severe odds, he made his way to the city of Botoshani, where he found a home for the little orphan boy.

Then with characteristic audacity he sent a coded message – via some Russian soldiers – to Jenny in Chernowitz, indicating where he was. For a quart of free vodka the Red Army men were happy to drive her all the way back to Botoshani, a good day's journey. Thus my mother and father were reunited: it was as if they had come back to one another out of hell.

Botoshani was crammed with people uprooted by the war, and was no place to settle. Soon Jenny found she was pregnant again, and Herman resolved to find quarters in Bucharest, the Romanian capital, two hundred miles distant. Travel was diffi-cult, with most civilian transport commandeered, but some Russian soldiers accepted a bribe to let the two hitch a ride on their military vehicles. Part of the way they rode on a loaded ammunition-truck and then clung desperately to a full petrol tanker, through the frequent air-raids of the retreating Germans.

Their first home in the devastated city was a share of a bare floor in a ruined apartment.

Thanks to the Russian 'liberation', Romania was now Communist-controlled.

March 2, 1945, Bucharest

A new baby girl was born to Jenny and Herman. This time rudimentary hospital care was available, and the new Frida was ushered into the world under sterile conditions. I am that second Frida.

How did I come to be Judy? This is what I will try to tell you –

how the many miracles which had happened to my parents
before I was born simply continued, and flowered into the
greater miracle of my becoming Judy, and finding my true
purpose in life.

CHAPTER ONE

The 'future of the country'

THE FIRST MEMORY I have of myself, aged three, is of running – running fast through a narrow passage, my father chasing me. Panting, I swarmed up the bent old sycamore tree at the very end of the yard, and jumped down to crouch on the roof of an abandoned storage shack. This was the safest refuge. No adult dared venture onto its thin cardboard roof.

Father, below, was stopped by a neighbour. As they chatted I sneaked down, ran into the house, and hid under a small table covered by a long cloth. A brief feeling of security came over me. Then up went the cloth, and father's finger signalled, 'Get out.'

I felt so small, weak and guilty, and yet I did not want a spanking. I *had* destroyed a piece of silk my father had woven, for which any necktie manufacturer would have paid the equivalent of £50.00. Besides, I had not succeeded in making even a single dress for my doll, as intended.

Sternly father hauled me out and placed me across his knee.

'Father, wait,' I wailed. 'I want to say something!'

'Well?'

'It's not fair! How can such a big man expect a little girl to be good all the time?'

Father's expression softened. He began to laugh, took me up in his arms and kissed me. How I savoured the sweet taste of my first victory in debate! I was so pleased with myself that this memory has always remained fresh in my mind.

Soon I was sent to nursery school. Almost all children went, because their mothers had to help in providing food. Though so young, we were strictly regimented, learning Communist Party songs for hours on end, songs in which the Party was the almighty Father, the provider for us children and for Mother Country. I learnt my lessons well, with immediate consequences.

One day a local shop received a delivery of cupcakes, a rare event. Excited, I ran with mother to get some, but an old childhood friend of hers chanced by. They started talking. I looked at the people rushing home, holding cupcakes as if they were fragile treasures. My taste-buds prompted me to hurry mother. After all, *she* knew the supply could not last more than an hour. Finally she gave me the money and sent me to stand in line, which by now stretched the length of a block. I thought of the instruction received in school. Without hesitation I quickly dashed to the front of the queue, ignoring frosty glances and angry comments, placed my money on the counter, and said, 'For all the money, cupcakes please.'

Ladies in the line scolded me, protesting loudly. One even started shaking me.

'Aren't you ashamed? Why can't you wait for your turn like everybody else?'

Very gravely I replied, 'Lady, I am the future of the country.'

They all fell silent. Politically speaking I was right. We were taught in school that 'children are the future of the country', so obviously to contradict me in public was to contradict the teachings of the Communist Party. No-one dared do that, fearing the informers who were present even in such lines.

When a neighbour told mother of my 'achievement' she started using me on a regular basis for shopping, especially after my only sister was born. By then I was four-and-a-half, and her appearance meant tough competition. She was very beautiful, and of course received all the attention. Exasperated, I exclaimed one day,

'You treat her like an angel born on earth!'

To this day I cannot remember who spoke to me about angels.

During September 1951, aged not quite seven, I attended school for the first time. Parents had to provide their child's uniform: a black long-sleeved dress with a white collar which opened at the front to take a big red ribbon. The hair had to be braided, also with red ribbons. It seemed very elegant to me, because it was the uniform worn by 'The Little School Girl', the main character of a Russian film. The Little School Girl was very nice, and very helpful, but above all, wise in Communist Party doctrine. We saw that film over and over again; the more we saw the film, the more we wanted to emulate her.

My initial enthusiasm soon wore off, and school came to feel like a strait-jacket. The roll was called every hour, though we had only one teacher, who knew us perfectly well. We all had to stand when called, when the teacher entered or went out. Each morning, hair, nails, shoes and uniforms were carefully inspected. We then went over the ABC book several times: it contained slogans and songs to the Party, which we faithfully learnt. Under this dull regime I very much looked forward to the first summer vacation, and had visions of playing all day long.

But my mother had other plans. We were going to move.

The 'house' in which we then lived consisted of two tiny rooms, and a small entrance hall. There was no plumbing. We had to carry all our water in from outside. Moreover the two lavatories located in the yard had to be shared with ten other families, and many quarrels arose over whose turn it was to clean them.

In the move, as in all our family activities, I had certain tasks to perform: in this case carrying pots and pans and brica-brac from the old place to our new one. By the end of the day, we were all exhausted. Nevertheless, mother still had to cook us an evening meal: to go to a restaurant was an extreme luxury which would have cost about half our monthly budget. So, while mother prepared everything, and my sister was happily asleep, father took me on his lap for a heart-to-heart chat.

'I am so proud of you. You helped us so much. This is the way I like you – a tough girl, not whining and feeble. I saw too many spoiled children dying in the concentration camps just because they didn't know how to handle hardships. Sometimes you may grumble, but one day you will be thankful for this experience.'

It may seem strange to most Western readers, who know suffering only at second hand, from television and newspapers, that so young a child should be warned of possible sorrows and catastrophes. I now feel it was very useful, but then I grumbled indeed, thinking I had good reason! When I was scarcely six years old my father made me clean my own shoes: soon after that I had to clean his too. Later he would send me on every kind of errand, telling me, 'You are not to give up until you have solved this problem as best you can. Never come home complaining "I couldn't do it".'

I never did. I would visit five or six shops in turn, until I got what I was sent for, and since my every success was praised I always tried to out-do what was expected of me. I wanted father to be proud of me.

Later I got used to his strictness, and understood that he was only trying to convey to me the technique of survival under a dictatorship.

Death of a dictator

March 1953

I vividly remember the day Stalin died. Everyone was affected in some way; some people were imprisoned, others released, but we all had one thing in common: everyone had to mourn. There were massive demonstrations all over the country. Whole schools and factories were obliged to march. The sirens began to wail as I was returning home from school, and at once everybody had to snap to attention. For about ten minutes we all froze. I stood in front of a wooden fence, waiting for the loudspeakers to dismiss us. As a symbol of life under Communism, this image can scarcely be improved on: staring at a blank fence, listening to news which may or may not be true, waiting to be told by some anonymous authority how to react to it. For that day the order was 'total mourning'.

Shortly afterwards, when the same Communist authorities allowed Stalin's crimes to be denounced, an interesting article appeared in the Romanian Communist magazine *Contemporanul*. This article recalled how children had wept at those mourning parades, but offered an explanation: the children were told to weep, and those who did not were slapped until tears came naturally.

Black market aspirins

Our new home was palatial by Romanian standards. Each of the twenty-six families sharing the house actually had running

22

cold water and a toilet in their little apartments, and each had a story of bribes, luck and long years of waiting.

My mother got ours through a militiaman who had been assigned a new flat in the centre of Bucharest, because of his position and connections: for the equivalent of £500 he arranged that our family should be allowed to occupy his former flat.

Its cool cellar was an important feature, since there were no refrigerators or frozen food. We had to buy winter provisions – enough wood, potatoes, apples, carrots, and onions to last about four months. Autumn was therefore a very difficult time for most people. They had to collect everything they could save during the year, and then stand in endless queues, since everyone wanted to buy at once. When we were lucky enough to get potatoes and carrots, we buried them in soil to keep over the winter.

Every time we needed some I had to go down to the cellar. I grew to hate that dark, cold, musty place, and detested digging for the precious vegetables with my bare hands, but when I complained mother commented, 'Be thankful God gave them to us. Others would be delighted to stand in your shoes. You just be grateful.'

I am truly grateful for her wisdom, because even at the best of times I was never completely free of problems. Then her words would ring in my memory, and I would deliberately consider how fortunate I was.

I realised I could wash myself while in Africa people thirsted terribly.

I enjoyed the sun while others lay in subterranean prisons.

I could read while sixty per cent of mankind was illiterate.

So I resolutely became thankful for everything – even illness, for there was a lesson in everything.

Sophisticated drugs, even aspirins, were only available on the black market. The state, being the only importer and authority in any field, had to certify all foreign drugs at a research institute. A certain budget was assigned to purchase dogs on which to experiment. Soon the researchers discovered that they could obtain dead dogs for much less than live ones, so they pocketed the handsome difference in price. When they reported, subsequently, that the new American drugs were useless, the proof was conclusive: every dog had died. Thus

Romania remained for years without so much as aspirins, peni-
cillin or streptomycin.

Like so many Romanian mothers, our mother helped us
through sickness the hard way – with mustard compresses or
warmed suction cups, and great, strong outpourings of love. As
she spent long sleepless nights near our sick-beds I realised that
God had given us this wonderful present: a *real* mother, whose
heart he filled with love for us. I promised, one day, that I
would try to do the same for my own children.

Traitor in bare feet

Less than a year later, trying to improve our standard of living,
mother found another, still better apartment for us. This was a
very rare achievement. The average Romanian family settles,
under Communism, for what it has – and may move once in
twenty years.

This move came about through our neighbours, Mr and Mrs
Luca. Mr Luca was an inventor who had refused to release his
discoveries in the field of propulsion unless the state would
increase his miserable salary. As a result he lost his job. Very
soon the Lucas, both over sixty, were entirely dependent on
the little food and fuel we and other neighbours could spare
them. He would even spend long hours in the park flying his
model helicopters, but only for boys willing to share their
lunches with him.

Eventually, heartbroken and defeated by the humiliation,
he begged for work under any conditions. At the time the
government badly needed his ideas, so he was once again
employed, and allowed to move into an attractive apartment
in central Bucharest. But he was not given any assurance on how
long he would be granted this special treatment.

Meanwhile their married daughter continued to live in our
neighbourhood, and since she was working, Mrs Luca used to
baby-sit for her. To reach her parents, each day their daughter
endured an hour's travel crammed in a tram, carrying the tiny

baby. Because our apartment was only five doors away from their daughter's, and because of the uncertainty of his new position, Mr Luca agreed to exchange with us if we would give them also the equivalent of two months' salary. To our delight, mother was able to arrange small loans from different friends.

For us it was truly a prophetic move out of the slums: the street was the only one in Romania named after Columbus. (What now seems interesting is that Columbus, also Jewish by birth, later became a Christian. He set out to discover the ten lost tribes of Israel but instead, discovered America, the country my father had dreamed of.)

Our new surroundings were beautiful. The building was originally custom-built for a rich family, then later used as an embassy. We were to live on the third floor in a single one of the five large rooms, plus a former maid's room with a balcony. On our arrival, however, a man confronted us and jeeringly informed father:

'You'll give me the room with the balcony.'

He did not have to say any more. His identity card, non-chalantly displayed, revealed that he belonged to the secret police. If we protested he could easily have landed father in prison for 'obstruction', so we yielded and gave him the balcony-room. Mother was crying. After all her efforts not only did we have to live in one room, but my sister and I had to sleep in one bed.

For the first time I saw 'people's democracy' in action, and realised that it neither served the people nor even resembled a democracy. For our 'guest', however, it was to be fatal! Soon after we had left that building he fell to his death from the very balcony he had coveted.

Next day, I tried to put out of my mind our disappointment and frustration in an effort to function normally. I played outside making new friends until stopped by two women. One asked me why I was barefoot. I will never forget her severe face and voice as she said, gripping my arm:

'Don't you know we have guests in the country? Go home at once and tell your mother to get you clean and put on your shoes!'

I took a better look at the two ladies and realised that I

ought to obey, quickly. They were some kind of officials, with white blouses and dark blue skirts made out of the material used only for militia uniforms. They referred to the international youth festival then taking place in Bucharest. From all over the world young people had come to be shown how prosperous Communist Romania was. The government was keen that the tourists would see only the show they had mounted, not shabby-looking natives – especially in this elegant quarter of the city. The whole situation resembled a joke that appeared about then:

Through a clerical error Stalin arrived in heaven. After inspecting it he commented to St Peter:

'I'd like to visit hell and see for myself if it's really as bad as you Christians insist.'

St Peter gave him a one-month tourist visa and Stalin set off. At the gates of hell two devils greeted him and drove Stalin around in a beautiful Cadillac. There were delightful entertainments: films, vodka, a circus, theatres, museums and hockey games. He had a ball.

When the month was over Stalin reluctantly returned to heaven and went straight to St Peter.

'I knew you Christians were lying,' he accused. 'I have now been to hell and have seen with my own eyes what a fine place it is. I want to go and live in hell.'

He got a permanent visa.

Again he arrived at the gates of hell and the same two devils were waiting for him. This time, however, they drove the other way. They threw Stalin into a cauldron of boiling water and started tormenting him with tridents.

'Help! Stop! Wait a minute. I must be in the wrong place,' cried Stalin. 'I wanted to get to hell. Is this hell?'

'This is hell, all right, comrade Stalin,' replied the devils.

'But I have been here before,' protested Stalin wildly, 'and I was given star treatment.'

Jeering, the devils answered: 'You were duped, Stalin. Last time you were here as a tourist.'

The penalty for telling this joke in Romania could be many years in prison, so in the most resigned way I obeyed those two officials.

That summer many parades were held in connection with the

festival in the round plaza by the park across from our house. At night there were plays in the open air, orchestras, dancing, and plenty of ice-cream.

Unfortunately it did not last. When the three-week festival finished, so did the fun.

My new school started soon after that. Before the Communist take-over it had been the biggest, best-known and most respected school in the country. Now, in its elegant main hall, we started each day with songs to the Party. One ran something like this: 'We thank the Party with all our heart/For everything it has done for us . . .'

For a while I tried to believe those songs, to get a slight sense of belonging and security; but even that feeling soon melted away like the rare ice-cream of the summer festival. The words of Communist songs simply did not reflect the reality of Communist life around me. Every time I dared ask a question about it at school I was sent out of class, to stand in the hallway for the rest of the hour. Communism, as I began to understand, twists and misuses everything to fit its theories and serve its propaganda, while punishing every non-conformist.

Even a little fairy-tale could not be left intact. We once staged, at school, the story of 'The Fussy Princess', who suffered so badly from insomnia that she could even feel a pea through twelve mattresses.

A servant-girl promised a cure if the Princess agreed to work in the kitchen. After one day, tired out from healthy exertion, the Princess was cured: she fell soundly asleep on a chair. Moral: 'Only those who work sleep soundly.'

I did not then suspect that a Party writer had given this dismal proletarian flavour to the classic Hans Andersen story in which a pea under twelve mattresses kept the Princess awake – thus proving her nobility.

But that happy and romantic ending of marrying the Prince, and later becoming Queen did not fit Communist doctrine. Neither did Shakespeare's 'Romeo and Juliet,' so it too was clumsily adapted. At the end, after both unfortunate lovers had died, instead of the mourning parents as in the original, a group of chanting boys and girls appeared holding sickles and hammers. Their song explained that such stupid deaths occurred only in Capitalist times: now youngsters of both sexes build socialism and no longer have the time to languish for love.

Everything that was filmed, staged, broadcast, or printed, first passed through the hands of our glum, finicky, eagle-eyed censors, so all we ever received was their humourless political interpretation of literature and art. On everything they left their dreary, solemn stamp.

Before the Party holidays we had weeks of rehearsals. We were marched and dragooned, and we shouted slogans until we were hoarse. It was all a well-planned confidence trick, staged for visitors. Western tourists reported what a happy people we were. They could not see the holes in our ill-made shoes, or hear the growls of our empty stomachs. Even the Rev. Johnson, Dean of Canterbury, declared after visiting Romania that our country was a model for the liquidation of unemployment.

'There exists not one redundant worker in Romania,' proclaimed this dignitary, and he was right. The moment someone was discovered to be unemployed, he was flung into prison to work there for nothing, on a starvation diet. This fear was quite adequate incentive for people to work very hard at keeping their jobs.

From the outside we may have looked and sounded happy, but we had rehearsed well; it was part of the script. The following is also part of the script, but censored from visitors' eyes.

A passport to jail

At five in the morning we were awakened by loud, insistent knocking on the door. Two tough, stony-faced plain-clothes men shoved their way in, showed mother their secret police I.D. cards, and announced that they had to search our house.

This is standard secret police procedure in Romania, at any time of day or night: no need for warrants or even a sensible reason. These two said they were 'looking for guns'. Clearly it was a ridiculous pretext for prying into the belongings of new tenants. No private citizen had had any arms since the general confiscation in 1947.

My sister and I were told to remain in bed, and so was

my father. The men threw everything on the floor in the middle of the room. They were furious when they could not find anti-Communist literature, Bibles, or other books published before 1945. Then they told my father to dress and go with them.

This was an arrest. Father had instructed us previously that if such a thing happened we were *not* to protest, weep or act nervously: unjust imprisonment was so common that children were carefully drilled in such matters, much as in the West they might be taught how to cross a street. In spite of our emotions we tried to look unperturbed. Mother said loudly, 'Time to get up, girls. Go and get yourselves ready for school.'

Usually I would scamper across the room to get my own clothes. Today mother brought them to my bedside, and as she bent over she whispered, 'Quick, go and fetch father's address-book from his bedside table. Hide it in your blouse, and on your way to school get rid of it.'

I understood why.

Names and addresses were evidence that one was 'a counter-revolutionary trying to organise a rebellion', and the secret police would arrest all those people whose names appeared on the list.

My father worked as a rural salesman for 'Adas', a complicated state-controlled operation which sells compulsory insurance. (One service it did not provide was insurance against mindless persecution, wrongful arrest, and illegal detention.) He was in the greatest danger because he kept a list of friendly peasants who would accommodate him when he was travelling. 'Adas' gave father an allowance for overnight hotel expenses, but he was obliged to stay with peasants as there were no hotels in the areas where he worked. For this the secret police could, and would, accuse him of conspiring with those peasants against the government. The awkward fact that there were no hotels would have had no influence on their conclusions.

If discovered, father was also technically guilty of pocketing the small difference between the hotel allowance and the amount the peasants charged him; it was also true that he would not have done this, had it not been 'recommended' by his immediate superior, who also took a share. It was not strictly honest, but what is the rule of honest conduct when upright men fall into the hands of a dishonest dictatorship?

Romania is an Orthodox country. In the Orthodox tradition there is a story that a monastery was attacked by robbers. Prompted by Christian love, the monks helped the bandits load the spoil on horseback. When the robbers were ready to leave, the abbot came running with a candlestick in his hands. 'You forgot to take this,' he panted. 'I apologise for not pointing to it earlier.' Then he turned to his brethren. 'And now let us enter our church and pray with the same zeal with which these men have stolen.'

Is this the normal conduct when one has to deal with robbers, or the exceptional, expected of saints only? Even in Romania to steal a purse is theft, and stealing a large sum is robbery, yet the state takes everything from everybody. This is termed 'the fulfilment of the lofty ideal of socialism'. In the pursuit of that ideal tailors have lost their shops, barbers their salons, poor peasants their sheep – yet it is 'sabotage' for the victim to try to get back even a small fraction of what the state has stolen. Starving peasants have been sentenced to twenty years in prison for 'stealing' small amounts of wheat from what had been their own field before the state confiscated it. My father could have received the same punishment for his 'betrayal' of state and people. The robbers were now law-givers and judges, so obviously the address-book had to get lost – fast.

I was very scared. Any mistake could have been fatal for my father, and none too pleasant for me. Cautiously, trying to conceal my shaking and fear, I managed to take the infamous book from its hiding place and slip it under my pullover. On the way to school I buried it deep in a rubbish bin, relieved and proud that, though barely nine, I could outwit the foxes, the secret police.

During the last class that day our teacher read a typical propaganda story about an orphan negro boy in New York, who earned his living as a window cleaner, working twenty floors up on the face of a Manhattan skyscraper, and constantly in danger of falling. At night he searched rubbish bins for left-overs to feed himself. By the end of the story the whole class was in tears, but for me it was even easier to sympathise with him. What was going to happen to my parents now? We, too, could be facing a long fall. I walked home full of sadness for his plight.

As I passed the rubbish bin in which I had hidden the address-book, I got an idea. If the black boy could look for food there, I could certainly retrieve father's book. Mother had not suggested I keep it, but I knew those were contacts father might need again. I rummaged around and found it.

At the door mother joined me and we set out at once for the nearest police station, where we suspected father might be held. We waited outside for hours, shivering in the night air: to go in and ask about him would not have been wise. All we wanted was a glimpse of him: if he was removed from that station perhaps we could follow and learn his destination.

At last, many miserable hours later, father appeared, alone. We were unbelievably fortunate. In many such cases people just disappeared, for years and years of prison. He told us he had been questioned the whole day long, without food. Nothing could be pinned on him, so this time they had let him go. I told him about our anxiety over the 'sabotage' charge which could have stemmed from the address book, and described my part in its disappearance. Father was naturally very pleased with our performance, and ignoring our frantic hushing he tried to cheer us up with a political joke.

'Our Prime Minister called for the Minister of Agriculture, and asked him: "Can you arrange for cows to produce five to ten calves, the same way as a cat has five to ten kittens?" This was the best idea he had had all week.

' "But this is against all the laws of nature!" protested the Minister for Agriculture.

'The Prime Minister drew himself up to his full height. "If you, as Minister, cannot persuade the cows to perform better, you are guilty of *sabotage!*" he shouted, and the poor Minister for Agriculture was led away to prison.'

Though only a joke, it was not far from the mindless reality in which we had to exist, so we laughed and felt happy and lucky to have survived another day of anguish. As we walked on father revealed that on many occasions during his business trips he had been held and questioned for hours, even days, but suggested that it was better for us not to think about it. However, while father was glad to have escaped imprisonment once again, for me there was trouble ahead.

31

Jewish, and proud of it

Romania had started offering cheap vacations on the coast of the Black Sea, and it was being discovered afresh by Western tourists. They came in big groups and some of them visited our school, which served as a show-piece. No matter what subject was being taught, they liked to observe us and then ask questions through a Romanian Party-approved interpreter. In preparation we were thoroughly drilled during the weekly political education period.

When asked, 'Where does your father work?' we had to parrot, 'In the labour field.'

To 'What exactly does he do?' we had to recite, 'He is working toward making socialism a reality in our country.'

Then, to spur us on to greater achievements, we would be told about Stakhanov, the champion of Soviet workers who regularly produced far above his quota and was presented as a legendary figure in all Communist countries. I remember the teacher once saying, 'Stakhanov has done all this out of love and gratitude toward the Red Army, our mother, and our father, the Communist Party. Now, to honour them, what would you like to be?'

'An orphan,' was my immediate reaction, but naturally I did not say it out loud. The other children probably had similar dangerous thoughts, for no one dared speak up. Finally the teacher had to tell us what to answer: 'A Stakhanovite.'

We were given to understand that we were expected to try and achieve at least as much as he did. For tourists, then, who asked, 'What do you want to be when you grow up?' the correct answer was, 'I want to be a Stakhanovite – a workers' champion.'

It still astounds me how supposedly sophisticated Westerners could be so gullible as to accept the 'spontaneous' answers which we swallowed and regurgitated on demand.

One day, during the political education hour, the school superintendent asked everyone, 'What nationality and religion are you and your parents?'

This caused everyone terrible confusion. What lay behind this question? What were we supposed to say? We had not been taught the correct answer to such a question! Make the wrong response, and you might be expelled from school or have your parents sacked from their jobs.

Fear and bewilderment suddenly descended on us like a dark and menacing cloud. It was pathetic to hear the answers hesitantly given: children, suddenly on their own, trying to work out what they should say to please authority, after years of being drilled in acceptable answers and attitudes.

'I am a Romanian . . .'

'I – I don't know what religion is . . .'

'We – um – we don't talk about religion at home . . .'

(That seemed safe. Many answered like that.)

'I have the same religion as my grandmother.'

'I am an evangelical Christian,' said one girl, and you could feel the air turn to ice around her.

As uneasy as the rest, I sat in my chair, knowing an answer would be demanded of me sooner or later, but dissatisfied with repeating any of those I had heard so far.

While others stammered and hesitated, I went over my scant religious experience. I remembered how my mother had gone to the temple and emerged with eyes full of tears. It was the day she remembered the dead in her family. There were many of them.

At other times she and father would fast the whole day. But there were also happy Jewish celebrations. We would carry miniature flags of the state of Israel, white with blue lines and the Star of David in the middle. On top of the flagstaff we would have a nice red apple, and in a hole cut in the apple we would place a small candle. This holiday is called Simchat Torah (Joy of the Torah), when religious Jews celebrate the end of the year-long reading from the Five Books of Moses. Then there was the happiness of Rosh Hashana (the Jewish New Year) and Succoth (the Feast of Tabernacles) when free cookies and drinks were passed around the temple.

One holiday, however, impressed me more than any other: Pesach (Passover). At Passover, father sat very gravely at the table and gave us his simplified version of the ancient traditional ritual. It went something like this:

'And now, children, let us thank God that we were rescued from slavery in Egypt. He guided us through the desert, he fed us and defended us from our enemies, and brought us to this day. Blessed be our Lord God, our powerful Saviour.'

Then we would ask, 'But Father, when were we slaves?'

'We were slaves in Egypt, and again in the concentration camps, and God rescued us from both. That is why we are celebrating today. This unleavened bread is in remembrance of those times.'

Thus I knew I was Jewish, but I did not know if my parents wanted me to say so. We were always cautioned about which matters were for public consumption, and which were to remain strictly in the family. Since my father's last arrest, I had become even more careful about what I said to strangers, or how I answered personal questions in school.

My name did not come up during that hour, but I knew it would the next day. I asked father what to answer. I will never forget what he told me, and how sad he looked as he replied, 'The Russians liberated us from concentration camp, from the hands of the Nazis. Then the Romanian Communists promised that never would there be discrimination against the Jews as long as they were in power. And now my child has to go through the same terror I suffered under the Nazis!'

I protested. 'Father, all they want to know is what religion we practise.'

'Yes, but I don't like that. When they start asking such questions, it doesn't smell good.'

'What am I going to answer?' I insisted.

He thought for a moment. Caution, anger, then decision showed in his expression. He said firmly, 'Listen, I endured a lot for being Jewish, but I am not ready to forsake my beliefs. So you stand up and say, "I am Jewish, and proud of being Jewish." '

It made a very strong impression on me that my father, who had suffered so much, would teach me to answer so courageously. I was *not* going to disappoint him. Next day, exactly as father had instructed me, I stood up and said,

'I am Jewish, and proud of being Jewish!'

I was numb with emotion and felt as if everyone around me had frozen. The teachers glanced at each other, but kept quiet for a few interminable seconds. Then they looked at me with shock and reproach. I looked back straight into their eyes. One teacher said, 'Fine, sit down.'

At the end of the day, the superintendent told me, 'Ask your father to come and see me tomorrow between ten and eleven.'

34

'But he is working. I do not know if he can – '

'Tell him he *has* to come.'

I went back to the classroom and burst into tears. My best friend, Gaby, put her arm around me, and walked me home. I waited downstairs, still crying, while Gaby went to tell my parents that I was not coming up unless they promised not to punish me. I was already acting as Communism wants its youth to act: never sure what is right or wrong. Very surprised, my parents listened to my story. They were sad, and worried, but not angry at me.

Next morning father and I saw the superintendent. She told him, 'We shall have to move your daughter to School Nineteen. This is a disciplinary measure we are obliged to take.'

She managed to convey that this was not her own choice: outspoken youngsters had to be sent to obscure schools, the ones not visited by tourists. We left her office feeling miserable. Father walked home with me, but we did not talk any more. It hurt too much.

Next day I started at School Nineteen. Everyone looked at me as if I were a peculiar animal. It was exactly as I had feared. In Romania, from kindergarten right up to the end of secondary school, each school year started in September with thirty or forty students per class. We came together every day for five or six hours, in the same classroom, for the entire school year, so we got to know each other very intimately. A new student was a rare event, and few left the class before the end of the year. This created real peer-pressure, and the shame of being moved in the middle of the year was almost unbearable.

I felt as cold and lifeless as the winter (1955) which then descended on us, the worst winter we had in fifty years.

CHAPTER TWO

Necessity . . . the best teacher

It snowed six feet overnight. Many basement-dwellers could not even get out of their house. Yet we had to buy bare necessities every day, so the second day after the blizzard I trudged through snow for several hours, making a round of stores, until I was frozen and exhausted, but I could find no bread at all. Fortunately I ended up not far from some friends' house, so I went in to warm up. They gave me a quarter of a loaf so that I should not return home empty-handed. This meant quite a sacrifice.

When I finally reached home I found not only my mother and sister but also our neighbours, the Dobels. Father was away on a work trip, as usual. They were all trying to get themselves warm, clustering round the small electric heater that mother had dug out from her store of secret treasures. She also shared all the food in the house.

Before the Communist takeover, the Dobels had been prominent in the high society of Bucharest, very rich and respected. Now the old couple had to live in one room, sharing the kitchen and toilet with four other families, and without access to a bathroom. They had been allowed to keep only a few pieces of furniture: these were indeed beautiful and testified to an opulent past. The light yellow lemonwood was artistically carved in a beautiful French provincial style. It was in their room that I first saw hand-carved crystals, and a Chinese statue of the Buddha which was at least one hundred years old when they had purchased it twenty years before. It was made of black porcelain and adorned with exquisite stones and pearls. Once Mrs Dobel showed me their bed-linen, embroidered with their initials: this was the epitome of luxury in Romania. She asked me not to tell a soul. If our 'guest' from the secret police had learnt of them he could have taken them without payment, but Mrs Dobel needed them just to survive. She sold them on the black market, piece by piece, since the state pension was barely enough to pay the rent for the room. She also told me that the villa they owned, which the Communists had taken away, was alone worth several million lei, enough for them to have lived happily for another fifty years.

The Dobels were of German descent, and not particularly keen on Jews. When we had first moved in they kept their distance from us. Now that the snow and the cold forced them into our room, near our heater, they became our adopted grandparents.

Both were refined and well-educated. I would certainly have liked to have such grandparents, especially since I never knew any of my own except my mother's mother. All the others died in concentration camps or pogroms during the Second World War.

Mr Dobel decided to coach me with my maths homework, so he came every afternoon and spent at least an hour with me. If I ever learned any geometry and algebra, it was only through his efforts to help me master the basics, which until then, I must confess, had been my bitter enemies.

Despite my new grandparents, these were dreary times. There was never quite enough food, practically no luxuries; and the shadow of possible arrest still hung over my father, even more so after my outspokenness. Fortunately my new classmates gradually came to accept my presence, and the bitter winter gave place to a bleak and chilly spring.

One source of pleasure, however, was our friendship with another couple of neighbours: Sofia and Barbu Popescu. They were both young, and had a darling baby girl, Anny. My sister and I used to fight to baby-sit for her, and mother spent many nights near her crib while she was sick. The Popescus offered to take me that summer to a village near Cluj, about three hundred miles from Bucharest, where Sofia's mother, Maria, lived. I eagerly accepted, and anxiously sought my parents' sanction: thankfully, they approved.

After twenty-four hours' travel we reached Maria's mountain village. It was quite a change for me. I was used to Bucharest's big railway station, and the trams and buses running outside. Here, however, there was only a wooden shed near the station, a scant refuge against the rain or snow.

We arrived after dark, when the whole village lay asleep. Occasionally carts pulled by oxen or a lean horse passed us on the muddy road, and one sleepy peasant agreed to give us a lift. The route to Maria's house was pitch dark, not one street light. I couldn't help thinking about another boasting from the Communist platform: the electrification of the rural areas. For years I had listened in school as my teachers proclaimed, 'Peasants now enjoy electricity, a luxury they have never had before.' Now we were travelling through the village – a twenty-minute ride – and all we saw were the four bulbs which lighted the railway station, which also served as the business centre of the village.

When we arrived Maria offered us milk which she had received only hours before as her share in the collective farm. I will never forget the taste of that warm, rich, bubbly milk, so different from any I had ever tasted. Maria told us why: to have more to sell to city consumers, the state watered the milk; hers was the real thing.

Next day the neighbouring children came to look me over, the girl from the great city. After that preliminary inspection they took me hiking in the mountains. It was enchanting: trees, sunbeams through the foliage, birds chirping. It felt so cosy! We gathered raspberries and washed them in clean, cold mountain-stream water. This was the first time I had ever picked them myself, and I came to realise how difficult it was to gather even a few ounces of that delicacy.

Another day I helped to harvest the wheat. I was so hungry and thirsty by lunchtime that bread, cheese, and water tasted like a banquet. Sitting in the shade was a delight, and when evening came I could hardly wait to tumble into bed.

Prayer and proof

One rainy day two of my new friends decided to go to the pictures. I would have liked to go along, but I had no money. Embarrassed, I told them I had to ask permission from my hostess and would join them inside if I got it. I turned around glumly, knowing that I could not possibly ask Maria for money. She had already sacrificed enough by feeding me. Walking sadly home I thought, 'At least I could *pray*. Maybe God can help me find some money.' I walked on, looking at the ground as I prayed. All of a sudden I stopped short: out of the mud stuck a very small corner of – a whole one leu note! I ran to a nearby drinking fountain, washed the note, pressed it to my jacket very gently so it would not disintegrate. Then I ran back to the cinema victoriously.

I could think of nothing but this apparent miracle – that I had got the money when I had prayed for it.

A few days later as I was dressing, I could not find my only clean pair of socks. When I asked Maria, she said, 'That's easy, dear. Just take a glass and whisper into it, "Glass, glass, dear glass, help me find . . ." – whatever you are looking for. Turn the glass upside down and start looking again, and soon you will be sure to find it.'

This sounded like peasant superstition to me, but, not wanting to insult her, I accepted the glass she gave me, went into a corner and made semblance of following her instructions. After putting the glass down, hardly able to hold back my chuckles, I sat on my bed and instead prayed silently to God. The logic was simple: if he helped me find money which I did not have, he surely could help me find the socks I did have!

I was interrupted by little Anny, rushing into the room chased by a chicken. She was laughing but exhausted, and came straight to me begging to be picked up. I took her in my arms. Her jacket pulled up – and out fell my socks. From that day on, when everything else failed I made prayer my 'secret helper'.

A very special washing-machine

On my return to Bucharest I found a pleasant improvement in our laundry routine. Laundry was always a very difficult task, not only in our family but all over Romania. Women took care of laundry and still do it by hand with a washing board. Laundry-day came once every three weeks and it took at least a day to wash a few towels, sheets, father's shirts and maybe a couple of dresses for us. Then it took two days to iron them. There were no wash-and-wears!

The washing itself was a torture. There were no protective

gloves on the market, so mother rubbed the clothes inch by inch in her bare hands. When we came home from school on laundry day, we would find her exhausted, hands almost raw from the crude soap and soda.

So the improvement in our laundry methods was a wonderful surprise – no, it was not a washing-machine: I would not see one of those until I went to the United States – the improvement was called Florica, and she was a washer-woman.

Florica was a gentle soul. She worked hard and never mixed in our petty quarrels, possibly because she was not much of a talker. One day over lunch, however, we managed to find out something about her.

She was obviously an educated woman; she used to work as a Morse Code operator, and had married one of her supervisors. For years she had attended church regularly, but did not become a full believer. One day, however, she was attracted by a very dedicated group of evangelical Christians, and became a practising member of their underground church. She therefore refused to work on Sundays and got into real trouble: she was fired from her job, and her husband, a convinced Communist, soon left her. She was not happy about it, but was ready to work as a washer-woman if this was what it took to prove her allegiance to God. We all loved and respected her; mother even accompanied her to a worship service, but she did not allow Florica to evangelise us. Unfortunately for us, after about a year her husband started following her to the underground church prayer meetings: he hoped to get credit for discovering a whole nest of 'enemies of the people'. She decided to leave Bucharest for another town, where her church friends directed her to hide with other believers. And so we lost our most 'trouble-free' washer-woman, but we remember her gracious nature to this day.

A dance for freedom

The order came through that we had to take part in an extra school activity. I registered for gymnastics.

Twice a week we would go to a gym on the other side of the city. This meant an expensive bus ticket. It must be understood that we had no cars or bicycles. We also had to provide our own uniform, and the special gymnastic slippers. Total cost: the equivalent of £60.00.

The slippers lasted six months, then the leather under my toes wore away completely. I used those slippers for two years, without missing a single lesson, not even in winter when we had to stop every ten minutes or so to rub our numb hands and toes, for the gymnasium was not heated at all. Our teacher was very talented, and taught us a combination of gymnastics and dance. I loved it.

Sometimes at home I would push the dinner-table aside, roll up the carpet and exercise on the bare parquet floor, my mother's pride. I should have paused to reflect on our neighbourhood: a Party official, Mr Cocor, lived in the flat below. One afternoon while I was practising, Mr Cocor's maid knocked on our door. Our one room was above his dining-room, and he complained that the squeaking floor bothered him. He threatened to use 'serious measures' if this went on.

After that mother hushed practically our every move. Soon, however, the elegant chauffeured car stopped picking up Mrs Cocor for her shopping, and Brindusha, their daughter, for school. We started seeing them—instead of their maid – in the regular neighbourhood queues for groceries. It was evident from their faces that Mr Cocor had been 'demoted' – that is, jailed. I felt sorry for them. I wanted to give them a few words of encouragement but found I could not. After all, he had made life even more difficult for us by restricting our movements in the only room we had, while he could easily have shifted to another room in his enormous apartment.

I did not know what to do . . . shun them, as they had shunned us, or befriend them when everybody seemed to avoid them? Should I be glad or sad? I could not decide and none of the neighbours dared to be the first. The Cocors were 'undesirables' now.

When the next summer vacation came, for the first time I was truly sorry, because it interrupted the gymnastics course. But I found something else to do – I entered a competition for a children's dancing class at 'The People's School of Art'. Out of over three hundred candidates, only thirty-five passed: I was among them!

My heart pounded with joy. I rushed back home shouting, 'I did it! I did it!'

My parents did not know what I was talking about. After I had sat down and got my breath back, I told them this was the school that prepared dancers for the National Folk Dancing Ensemble of Romania – the one going abroad!

But becoming a famous dancer, touring the West, and defecting, was a dream that never came true for me. After a year's study at The People's School of Art the authorities decided there were enough dancers for the time being and the school closed down. It was bitter news for me: no glamour, no freedom, not even a hope. For a while I was crushed.

CHAPTER THREE

The seeds of revolt

While I was still at junior school we moved yet again. My mother had found another, still better home for us. This time she handled the transition really well by keeping the details very secret. The lady with whom we were exchanging apartments, Mrs Jonescu, did not tell anybody either. Mother arranged to have Mrs Jonescu's apartment painted while she was still living there, to prevent another secret police officer from helping himself to our new home.

Though mother's dreams had finally come true, the move ate up all our savings. Other projects had to be shelved, and we scrimped hard to restore some kind of financial balance. Then almost at once, when we could least afford it, father lost his job. The directors wanted someone with full Party allegiance. So, from selling insurance, my father turned to rubber-boot repairing – just a reminder of the Party's role in our lives.

Due to my forced move from one school to another, I had not been made a Pioneer, which is an essential stage in the Communist education system. In secondary school we would be obliged to become members of the Youth Union, another arm of the Communist Party: therefore, we had first to become Pioneers. So, willing or unwilling, I was made a Pioneer that year, which was like being accepted into a sorority two weeks before graduation in the last year of college. So ended the five good years during which I had escaped additional indoctrination sessions. Now I would have to shout slogans like FOR THE CAUSE OF LENIN AND STALIN FORWARD and DOWN WITH THE AMERICAN CAPITALISTS. We were the young puppets of the Communist Party.

As soon as I became a Pioneer I was invited to a yearly carnival at the Pioneers' Palace in Bucharest. This very beautiful retreat for former Romanian royalty had been turned into a

43

recreational facility for youngsters. There could be no stronger bait to make us desire to become Pioneers. In our drab, crowded homes we all dreamt about the Palace, even though most of us detested the other duties of the Pioneers.

I had to prepare a costume. Mother wanted me to make a big splash, so she asked the help of Mrs Jonescu, a talented dressmaker. There were no costumes to be bought or rented, so from ordinary material she created a long pink dress and a hat, and added lots of paper flowers as decoration. A wire hoop transformed the dress into a crinoline fit for a duchess. I stood before the mirror in admiration, ready for the costume contest.

There were at least one hundred costumed dancers at that carnival. When I heard that I had been chosen as one of the finalists, I hopped up and down with excitement. However, when the panel of judges asked what my costume represented, I remembered my fantasies and not my common sense. 'A duchess,' I chirped. All the judges frowned at me. Until then, everyone had seemed sure that I was going to receive first prize, but at that moment I realised my big mistake: in this society 'duchess' stood for 'enemy of the people'. Had I said 'baroque' or perhaps 'antique costume' I would surely have had some kind of award, but now I got nothing; not even a consolation prize.

One day in our natural science class we were shown a microscope for the first time. Its function was explained to us, and we were allowed to examine different objects with it.

First the teacher showed us a razor blade and a needle. Under the microscope they looked as uneven as a saw, but the sting of a bee appeared completely polished and straight. The finest thread from our factories looked like a rope, with hairs fraying out on all sides, whereas the thread made by the silkworm was perfectly even. Every man-made circle we examined was irregular: only the circles on the wings of butterflies were perfect.

When the teacher left the room quite a discussion arose. We jostled each other to get one more look through the microscope. We compared again the natural and the artificial objects. One boy simply commented, 'It takes quite a bit of intelligence to produce a needle and a blade; but since nature's works are so superior, then a higher intelligence must exist behind nature.'

At the end of the next lesson a girl had the courage to suggest this conclusion to the teacher.

'We teach no religion in our schools,' she replied abruptly. She turned to stalk out, and in doing so bumped against the desk, overturning the little microscope. Was it involuntary, or a deliberate gesture expressing her true feelings?

The contrast grew between my home life and my public one under the eye of the authorities. Sometimes they clashed violently. By that time I was thirteen years old, and I noticed my parents repeating more and more often a phrase from the Passover service: 'Shana haba be Yerushalaim!' – the Hebrew for 'Next year in Jerusalem!' This filtered deeply into my consciousness and I saw it as the ideal solution to all our problems.

I knew, of course, that Israel existed in fact, as a nation, the modern Jewish hope and ideal – and from the distant traditional past I was aware that Judaism was basically a Messianic faith.

A lot for a girl of thirteen to absorb and straighten out in her mind? Yes, and I don't claim to have been a wonder-child who achieved a synthesis of intellectual and spiritual ideas and yearnings. But, thanks to my father, I do recall most vividly my feeling of kinship with the ancient Israelites who escaped from Egypt and the burden of slavery. I had no difficulty in seeing the parallel between servitude then and life now under Communism. I knew without doubt that I had to escape from the strangling grip of Communism, and Israel became our magnetic dream-land.

I also wondered when the Messiah, the hope which had sustained the Jewish people for almost six thousand years, was going to arrive, and deliver Jews and non-Jews alike from the horror, boredom and crazy frustration of Communist existence. For me this question had daily immediacy.

There was a school which prepared dancers for the Opera House. One had to be no more than eight years old in order to join. Another vital qualification was written proof that one's parents owned no real estate. (How could they? It had all been confiscated in 1947, yet the farce must be played to the end.)

I was anxious to find a place in that school for my sister, then nearly eight. So, one morning, mother and I went to court for the 'no-real-estate' certificate.

The officer in question was not there, and no-one else was

45

prepared to issue the document. I tried to persuade the militia officer on duty that the document was the important thing – not who issued it. He scarcely glanced up from his paperwork, merely responding:

'Get out of here.'

Before my mother could shut me up, I angrily snapped back at him.

'This is the only chance my sister has this year – or any year – to enter that school. It's only a formality, anyhow! Why can't you be reasonable and help me?'

My mother, usually so capable of taking command of any situation, was stunned into silence by my outburst.

'I just don't feel like it,' the officer replied.

'You can't do that to me!' I raged. 'What right have you got "not to feel like it"? By preventing my sister from joining that school, you may be robbing Romania of a great dancer, cheating the glorious Party of another achievement – you *don't* have the right! Who's in charge of this place, anyhow?'

The holy words about the Party brought a quick pallor to his mean face. Then, realising who was confronting him, he replied calmly:

'I will show you what rights I have.' He signalled another militia-man nearby. 'Take her to the ice-box' (the cellar).

The militia-man grabbed me and started shoving me out of the room towards the stairs. My unthinking defiance evaporated at once. I craved forgiveness. I had never been so scared in my life. I could spend years and years down below without even coming before a judge. All this loathsome militia officer had to say was that I had 'misbehaved', and I could have been locked up and abandoned, just like that.

The officer, his streak of cruelty satisfied, finally let me go.

After that experience I was careful to avoid even jay-walking, fearing any confrontation whatsoever with militiamen. When I saw them, I saw devils. A neighbour confided that even the traffic police reserved a certain number of hours for the interrogation and beating of prisoners – he knew, he worked as an electrician for the militia.

Yet there must have been some inextinguishable spark of rebellion in me. Before long I was engaged in still another one-girl protest demonstration.

'How can you be such an idiot, you over there?' yelled 'Mrs' comrade-teacher Sergey at one of my classmates, up-braiding him for a petty mistake.

I protested that there was no reason to talk like that. I would not have intervened, had my classmate been able to handle such abuse, but he was a short, skinny Jewish boy, one year younger than the rest of us, extremely insecure. Yet he was very bright. But my reaction was quite futile. I still had not realised that it was dangerous – almost insane – to demand justice in Romania. Comrade Sergey became furious.

'Who asked your opinion? I'll get you for that!' And she did. Since it was just a few days before the end of the school year, she changed my citizenship rating for the whole year to six. The grades ran from one to ten, but, in citizenship, anything below nine meant 'Untameable – constant nuisance'. At first I had had a ten or a nine. When I was forcibly moved from one school to the other, the teacher had changed my grade to seven to justify it. Now this six was like writing 'hardened delinquent' on my record.

When I had to register for secondary school, the counsellor looked at my papers, then at me, wondering.

'You seem such a good girl. Why have you got a six in citizenship?'

I told her the story. She believed me and accepted my application. It was a true act of mercy on her part.

The wrong connections, the right friends

Three full days of mind-numbing exams followed.

I scored an 8.33 average, a good B – yet did not qualify for secondary school. There was no appeal. The reasons were cruelly obvious – and I felt enmeshed in a huge clinging spider's web.

Somewhere on the records I was identified as the girl who ran about barefoot in front of foreigners; who, proud to be Jewish, had been moved to School 19; who did not show proper respect to a militia officer; and who defended a fellow-Jew in class. In the mighty fantasy of imaginary guilt which is

Communist administration, I was probably also cross-referenced as the daughter of a man arrested several times and so cunning that nothing could be proved against him – though, if arrested, surely he had to be guilty of something; a man who gave up his job in state insurance rather than seek membership in the Communist Party.

In other words, had my father been a factory-worker, a former collective-farm peasant legitimately moved to the city, or best of all a Party member, I could have entered any secondary school just by scoring an average of five. My fault lay in thinking problems out and having the wrong kind of parents, instead of being a dullard with impeccable proletarian forbears. And yet, looking at the respected fathers of Communism I was really puzzled: Marx's father was a wealthy lawyer, Engels' a factory owner, Lenin's a nobleman, and Trotsky's a rich farmer! None of them had a 'healthy social origin'. There was no way we could question this inconsistency but I hoped that, one day, I could use this precedent for help.

The school year started. Suddenly cut off from all my friends, I became confused and depressed. To help me, father took me into 'his' shop daily in return for a 'salary' out of his own pocket. One day I was in there by myself. A young man, not much older than I, came in for a kind of sandal we did not have in stock. As I made up a special order for him he said, 'You remind me of Clara, my neighbour. You should meet her.' To be polite I answered, 'Gladly, when you pick up the sandals.'

We met and became friends. We were both almost fifteen years old. Clara was Jewish too, so we went to the Temple together to celebrate the Jewish New Year.

For us youngsters, the Holy Days were only social events. We could not participate in the religious rituals since the reading was in Hebrew and we had had no opportunity to study it. There were, however, some books with translations, and once, glancing through the pages, I found this prayer: 'Blessed be thou, God, the king of the universe, *that thou hast not made me a woman.*' I could not see anything wrong with being a woman. My mother was one and I was looking forward to womanhood.

I saw the Torah being solemnly taken out of a closet. These were the scrolls with the laws of Moses. They were draped in silk and velvet, and adorned with silver. When borne around the temple, everybody kissed them, but I had no idea what this sacred book contained. Neither did I know why my mother went to special prayers for the dead. Were the dead gone forever? Then what was the sense of praying for them? Or else maybe they were alive somewhere? I would have liked to talk about all this. There were so many dead in our family.

There was no one to enlighten me, so instead I joined Clara's crowd of youngsters in the temple yard. One of them, a very handsome boy named Bruno, asked me to be his guest at a restaurant with a group of other boys and girls.

I was overwhelmed! It was the first time I had been asked: my first date! I wore my one and only 'after-five' dress, and as a special favour my parents allowed me to return after 10 p.m. Like all the other girls, Clara and I ate at home beforehand, knowing that the boys could only afford cold drinks or ice-cream.

Everything about the restaurant enchanted me, especially the orchestra which was playing soft, romantic Italian songs. I danced every dance with Bruno. He walked me home, both of us on cloud nine. We became inseparable friends.

After finishing secondary school, Bruno had taken the entrance exam for medical school, but had been turned down because of his parents' non-Communist background. Eventually he was accepted for veterinary college. That was still something, even if it wasn't exactly what he had wanted. But for me there were no openings. Clara realised how unhappy I was about this, and one day she suggested, 'Why don't you go back to school?'

I looked at her rather sourly. 'But you know I couldn't pass the entrance exam.'

'You only tried it once. Try again!'

'On my own? Study all that stuff on my own? Impossible, I've never been a bookworm.'

'You'll just have to become one,' she insisted, 'and the sooner the better. Just think: when we finish secondary school and go on to university, you'll be completely left out.'

That did it. I started to study by myself, very hard.

In the summer of 1960 I sat the exams at the same school as Clara, and passed. I had somehow slipped through the web of prejudice and obstruction – for I was sure I had done the exams just as well previously as this time.

I could not wait to get into school again, but my enthusiasm began to cool off on the very first day. A review of impressions will explain why: Inspection of shoes, uniforms, hair, nails, just as if we were in kindergarten; boys' hair crew-cut; fifteen to seventeen year old girls in pigtails, no rings, pendants, or nylons (who could afford nylons anyway? When available, one pair cost anywhere from £40.00 to £100.00); special permission required to change desk-partners; a maths teacher like a prison warden; a sports teacher nicknamed Bismarck. As bad as he was, the maths teacher was a tamed lion compared to Bismarck.

Our Russian teacher however was a very good-looking young lady and I liked her very much. She had just finished at the Maxim Gorky Institute in Bucharest, which prepared only Russian-language teachers. Her Russian was very good, but her Romanian was not. How could that be? The explanation is simple: she came from the north-eastern part of Romania, which had been annexed by Russia immediately after the Second World War. Since then, more and more Slavic words had been introduced into the local Romanian dialect, and the population compelled to write in Slavic, instead of Latin characters. The Moldavian language was thus forced into birth, and the whole area called the Moldavian Soviet Socialist Republic. What she spoke could hardly be described as Romanian, though her parents were Romanian and she herself was born and raised as such until the Russian takeover.

I was good at languages and could manage the other subjects too, but there was one that seemed impossible: scientific socialism. Nobody else liked it either. For this course we had to study, and practically memorise, the speeches of the Romanian as well as the Soviet Party leaders. It looked like every other day a congress was held for different branches of industry and agriculture. Leading figures spoke on all Party and general holidays. The teacher insisted that we know the main idea in every speech, but that was most difficult: there was none. The speeches merely enumerated facts and figures wrapped around in clouds of verbiage. It sounded as if the speakers were practising their vocabulary, showing off how many new words they had learnt since their last speech. I congratulated myself on one matter, though: before the first hour of scientific socialism I had moved from the first to the back row. At least I could put my head on the desk and doze off for short periods.

There were some good people on the staff – one particularly delightful English teacher had studied at Oxford University – but they could not significantly ease the pervading, stifling atmosphere of oppression and severity. The object of Romanian education was not to prepare pupils to be able to make reasoned and independent judgements, but on the contrary to mould them to depend on the Communist Party and to accept its most unreasonable claims and demands without question.

CHAPTER FOUR

Michael

Every day of that school year seemed like walking on a tightrope. I would come home with terrible headaches wondering how much longer I would be able to stand the pressure. Talking to Clara was no consolation. She believed there was a solution: learning to live with it, of course. But I had known for some time that there was something insanely wrong with the system under which we lived, and that it did not have to be endured. Unconsciously I was already taking the first steps towards escape, for through my friend Bruno I was about to meet Michael.

It happened very casually. Clara and Bruno, who sometimes worked as film 'extras', met a young man at the set. They described him excitedly as 'the most well-read and intelligent ever!' A few days later Bruno introduced me to him.

From the beginning I sensed that Michael was strangely and subtly different from us, but on our next encounter he proved to be truly more than met our eyes.

Bruno and I were invited to an 'exclusive' party so we had to ask special permission from the host to bring Michael along. The evening started pleasantly, with Michael and Bruno exchanging opinions on books they had both read. To stand next to Bruno, my well-groomed friend, was quite unflattering for Michael, so modest in appearance, dowdy, unglamorous, and uncombed. However, once he started speaking he was captivating.

At the party we left Michael on his own for quite a while. When I went to see if he had made any friends I found him in a corner, talking to the least attractive girl there. I did not know her name, but I had seen her at other parties before, always alone, always shunned. I felt sorry for Michael and was ready to return to my cheerful friends when I noticed our host taking Michael to task.

It transpired that this girl had not been invited, and our

rude host was asking her to leave. Quietly, even meekly, Michael tried to intercede but our host was too full of himself to back down. In a gesture I can never forget, Michael took the girl's hand and said, 'If she leaves, then I leave too.'

I was amazed that no one appreciated Michael's beautiful gesture. Suddenly, looking round the circle of embarrassed faces, I could stand it no longer.

'He is my guest, if he leaves I'm going with him!'

I was generally considered the life of the party. I had expected that one by one all the other guests would take my side and leave as well. Instead, I saw them gaping open-mouthed at the girl, Michael and me. I went straight to Bruno, dragging him by the hand from the midst of his admirers and we stormed out the room.

'I'll explain later,' was all I told my bewildered escort. Once outside, I expressed all my admiration of Michael's gallantry.

'It was the least I could do for her,' he replied. 'I have often been thrown out of schools and meetings, while my closest friends stood by silently. It was refreshing to be able to help a fellow outcast!' He excused himself and took the girl home.

In that glimpse of Michael's strength of character I began to understand the meaning of friendship. After that Bruno and I frequently invited Michael out. It was always an enriching experience.

Spring, summer, autumn, winter: sunshine on fruit trees in bloom, rushing warm showers, dark cold rainy days, leaves turning red, drifts of fluffy snow flakes – all that beauty in nature, but who had time to indulge in its contemplation?

Every week, it seemed, another Jewish boy or girl left our class, another family had left for Israel, invariably after long and tortuous delays and applications.

There was probably not a single Jew who did not yearn to go to Israel, though the Communists mounted one propaganda campaign after another to persuade everyone to stay in Romania. A joke went the rounds about a Jewish Communist who addressed such a meeting. 'Don't go to Israel,' he insisted. 'It is a country of capitalists who are bound to exploit you. You go to buy a sack of onions and they might cheat you, giving you a sack of oranges instead. Keep right away from Israel.'

And beating his breast he finished with, 'Here is happiness! Here is freedom! Here is joy!'

After the meeting a friend told him, 'You were really good. You spoke marvellously. You're a born leader, but why did you beat your breast continually as you told us, "Here is freedom"?' The speaker answered, 'I was beating the pocket where I keep my passport – with my visa for Israel.'

We received letters and photographs from Israel. The pictures showed well-dressed people, and the letters described the pleasure of seeing uncensored films from America, France and Italy, and of being able to buy records by our favourite singers: Pat Boone, Paul Anka and Elvis. But this was not enough to satisfy me. I wanted to hear about their joy in living freely in the country of millennial Jewish dreams.

The Western reader is entitled to ask why we were allowed, in this regimented society, to receive such mail at all. Anyone who has lived under Communism knows the answer: in this way, the secret police, having copied and filed the letters before they were delivered to us, had something damning on us in their archives. If you think that is being paranoid, you are absolutely right. Communism thinks paranoiacally, creates paranoids, and manipulates them to its own advantage. It is as diabolically simple as that.

In the cold winter of 1961, Bruno's family suddenly received approval to leave for Israel. What for them was pure happiness was a terrible blow to me. Who would take me now on long strolls under the stars, recite poetry for me, and sing me romantic songs? He was my first love . . .

Bruno's family were given ten to fifteen days to get ready. They had to produce a certificate from the telephone company showing they owed nothing, even though they never had a telephone; they had to paint their house, even if it had been painted a few weeks before; they had to pay two years' rent in advance; they had to prove they held no library books, and so on and so on. To obtain these certificates quickly, a bribe was needed for every one of the clerks involved.

Then came the hardest part.

With all certificates on hand they applied for a plane reservation. By then at least ten days had passed, and it usually took three to four weeks to get a seat on a plane or train. In many cases people who had not left by the fourteenth day were denied exit, but their apartments, belongings, jobs and money were not returned.

I did not see Bruno for more than a week. When he came he looked exhausted but happy. He took me to visit Michael, who lived in an attic, a tiny room right under the roof. The floor was bare. There were two narrow beds, a cupboard full of books, a desk and a chair. Another young man shared the room with Michael.

By now I really liked Michael. Bruno knew he would have a good influence on me, so he asked him to act as my older brother. Michael agreed, adding:

'I wish I were you in your place. Promise you will not forget us.'

Before leaving, Bruno's parents held a big party, by Romanian standards. They too were living in an attic – five people in one tiny room – on Victory Road, the very centre of Bucharest. They had been there for ten years, expecting to leave any day. Finally it had happened. In honour of the occasion they bought a chicken, so we had chicken soup. Then the six of us *ate the whole chicken*. This was the first time in my life I had seen an entire chicken eaten at one meal. Once or twice a year, my mother would also buy a chicken but when she did she made it last a week. (No wonder a Romanian proverb ran: If a poor Jew eats a chicken, either he or the chicken must be sick).

Next morning Bruno and his family departed. I took out my handkerchief and waved and waved until the last coach in the train had disappeared. Then it occurred to me that I might never see Bruno again, never know freedom, and this brought a flood of bitter tears.

Pastor in prison

One Sunday morning I went to visit Michael. He had been feeling depressed, and was glad to welcome me. The Romanian Philharmonic Orchestra was playing on his radio and we talked about his family.

Michael's father was a pastor. For a moment I felt uneasy,

not knowing how to put it, then I blurted out:

'Didn't Bruno tell me that you were Jewish?'

'Yes, I am.'

'Then how can your father be a pastor?'

'We are Jews who believe in Christ as our Lord and Saviour.'

I was shocked, and didn't attempt to conceal it.

'How can a Jew believe in Christ?'

'Very simple,' answered Michael. 'Christ was Jewish too. It is more of a wonder that so many millions of non-Jews have become Christians – that is, they have accepted a basically Jewish religion. By becoming Christians we Jews stick to the most ancient traditions of our nation. Christ is our longed-for Messiah.'

If it was true, I was disappointed to hear it. I had hoped that the Messiah would save my mother from standing in queues, my father from the constant fear of arrest: in a word, would save us all from Communism. And as a special favour to the Jewish people, I had hoped that, when he came, we should all be able to breathe freely in Israel. Now I learnt that he had lived on earth two thousand years before, and that nothing better was going to happen.

I expressed my dismay, but Michael pursued his own line of thought.

'Jesus said, "I am not sent but unto the lost sheep of Israel," and "Salvation is of the Jews." '

This was question-and-answer of an entirely different kind from the Party-serving game we had to play at school. In Michael I sensed a mature conviction reached by personal spiritual experience and sacrifice; I saw a human being unafraid of the state machine which crushed opposition in general and religious adversaries in particular. I admired his courage, but his faith in Christ was deeply disturbing. I tried to find out about his parents.

'My father's in prison.'

'What for?'

He looked automatically out through the window, cautious that the secret police agents might overhear. He lowered his voice.

'For his faith. He is an extraordinary man. Here, I've got a picture of him.'

A tall, handsome man. Beside him stood a little lady, barely higher than his elbow.

'Your mother?'

'Yes. She was also in prison, and then was sent to a slave-labour camp for being his wife and for having continued father's church work. After three years of hard labour, hunger and misery, she was released. Father spent eight and a half years in prison. Then he had two and a half years with us. Not long ago he was re-arrested.' He stopped, trying to control the emotion this painful memory aroused.

'We don't know if he will survive this time. He's become very ill, yet we are not allowed to see him or send any food parcels or medicine. Even if we were allowed, we couldn't afford it. My mother was denied the right to work. Neither am I permitted to have a job, or study. Recently, on orders from the Party, I was expelled from theological seminary.'

'I'm sorry to hear that.'

'You shouldn't be. They weren't teaching us pure religion anyhow. It was a Communist interpretation and that place was miserable. On the first day we were each given a big canvas sack, and told to go out and collect hay to stuff it. This was to be our mattress. To sleep on such a bed, thirty boys in a room, living on a corn and bean diet, did not make the seminary the nicest place to be. Besides, we had no access to basic theological books. All we could get were those interpreted from the Marxists' materialist point of view.'

As part of the confidence-trick played on the West concerning 'religious freedom' in Romania, Michael explained, the Government wanted representation on the World Council of Churches. The existence of seminaries was, apparently, accepted by the Council as a proof of religious tolerance by the country concerned, and Council membership could ensue. This is how the godless could gain a respected voice in the Council.

'But not everybody in religious circles understands that.' Michael warmed to his theme. 'Cocooned in free lands, Christians tend to accept matters at face value – and an Iron Curtain delegate at a religious conference in the West means to them that Communist persecution of believers is obviously exaggerated. For instance, the Baptist seminary produces five or six pastors annually, for more than a hundred thousand Baptist believers who are scattered all over the country.' He grinned. 'This isn't an accepted level of productivity in any other area of Romanian industry!

'At the only Lutheran seminary in Romania, the one I attended, all the courses are held in German. Part of the technique is that of obstruction: it ensures that most students are discouraged from applying. Those who persist in attending, in spite of the poor conditions there, are continually urged to renounce their calling voluntarily, otherwise, quite coincidentally, their parents, relatives or friends might lose their jobs, apartments, etc. In my case, since my father was already in prison, and my mother was denied the right to work, I was simply thrown out.'

I asked about his future plans.

He hesitated, then with a peaceful smile replied, 'I don't know. God will show me. I just hope that one day I will also be able to escape from this country in order to become useful somewhere.'

Lowering my voice, I confided in him.

'A few days ago my parents and I made a new request to leave for Israel.'

'Just like that?'

'Well, not exactly. When we lined up in the freezing cold across from the militia H.Q. at 10.00 p.m. there were already about twenty people, and more were arriving every minute. Around midnight, a sweeping-machine was sent to turn its water-sprinklers on us. Some were so drenched that they had to leave, shivering, but nobody dared protest for fear of informers. We stayed there the whole night. Finally, at 7.00 a.m., my father, mother and I were admitted among the lucky one hundred. The rest, at least two hundred, were sent home.'

'My parents and I also made a request,' said Michael, 'at least two and a half years ago, but there is no chance of it getting through, because father is in prison. I don't even know if he is dead or alive.'

'How can you consider your father's death so calmly?'

'My father loses nothing by dying. For a Christian, it is gain; he goes to heaven where he will live in eternal happiness. In any case, father could never be really happy in this world. He is a Don Quixote type, always ready to fight even when the chance of winning is zero.'

People began to arrive, greeting Michael, then going on into the next room, his mother's. Among them were a Mr and Mrs Levy, whom Michael addressed as uncle and aunt. They talked to him with deep affection, as if they were really relatives. Michael introduced me: at this first casual encounter I had not the faintest idea what a crucial role they would play in my life. Michael told me that they were among the very few who constantly risked their freedom by helping Michael· and his mother survive while the father was in prison.

I wanted to know who all these visitors were. By then Michael and I had exchanged enough information to have each other imprisoned, had either been an informer. Yet there was still a hesitation on his part, and it was only after a very searching look that he finally confided a prayer meeting was about to take place in the next room. Would I like to attend?

I was flattered by his trust, but not yet ready to make a commitment, so I left.

Though outwardly I resisted the religious aspect, Michael's words planted deep in my heart and soul something even more precious than the desire to escape from the Party's 'paradise'. I was in the slow, inevitable, barely perceptible process of finding a purpose in my life, and, like Michael, a way toward an inner paradise of my own.

The opportunist

Not long afterward, Michael took me to visit someone who was in a different kind of prison – that of conformity. Jon was one of Romania's leading (and therefore Party-approved) writers. As customary in Romania, we wanted to offer him a gift, so we stopped at Bucharest's one and only supermarket, a very special place where only tourists and high party officials could afford to shop.

On a shelf we saw a plastic bag of imported frozen peaches. Romania had peaches only between July and September. Now it was March. Oh, yes, the picture on the package was very tempting, but I begged Michael not to buy it; it was outrageously expensive – twenty-five lei for one pound of peaches, the equivalent of a whole day's work. He explained:

'Yesterday we sold two pullovers which my uncle in France sent us. I feel rich! Besides, I've never had a chance to take you out before, and I don't know if I will ever have the money to do it again. So I'm going to splurge today!' It was a rare outburst of joy in Michael's usually serious and controlled mood. How could I get angry with him? I was glad he could forget his worries for a while.

Bearing the precious peaches we arrived at Jon's pleasant office. The sun streamed in on the neat rows of books behind his polished desk. Jon welcomed us cordially, but there seemed a slight tension in his manner as he shook hands and led us to comfortable chairs. He sat down behind his desk and leant his elbows on it: the desk apparently gave him confidence.

Michael talked about Jon's writing, reproaching him that it made no sense to philosophise and offer a moral point of view without presenting a standard of morals. I was listening from a corner while looking over some foreign magazines available only to the Party's chosen few. This was the only privilege for which I envied Jon. Michael continued:

'That's your big chance to influence the many people who read your articles. Implicitly, at least, you can present the moral principles Christ taught.'

'But I do not believe in Christ, in life everlasting, and in all the other myths of Christianity,' was Jon's loud response. He obviously made this textbook statement fortissimo for the benefit of whoever was listening, via monitoring bugs concealed in his office.

'If you don't believe in Christ, take Plato seriously,' insisted Michael. 'He said that writers must be like priests, because they form people's souls. Do you know the story about the bad writer who found himself in hell? A murderer and an arms dealer were consigned to suffer with him. First the murderer was taken and set to pump a vast pair of bellows, fanning the infernal blaze. When he slackened, he was whipped with knotted cords. The arms dealer was ordered to stoke the fires, carrying heavy loads of coal right into the furnaces. When he slowed he was lashed with leather thongs. The writer, however, was placed for ever in the centre of the inferno, to distribute the coal evenly. Whenever his concentration slackened he was scourged with metal rods. Naturally he complained at this treatment: he had to admit he had taught men abominable things, but he wondered why he should suffer so much more intensely than a murderer?

'A devil explained, "It is true these men are murderers, but once dead they will commit no more evil, whereas you have left your writings on earth. People will continue to read them and be inspired to horrible deeds. Your punishment has to be that much more severe." '

'Preachers' stories!' answered Jon scornfully. 'You must have heard that from your father. *We* write according to the teachings of Marxism-Leninism.'

Realizing how hopeless Jon was, Michael changed the subject by producing the peaches. We started eating them with tooth-picks. They tasted like icicles, and I cannot say I enjoyed them, but I shall never forget them either! It was the one and only time I ate anything frozen in Romania.

In the tram on our way home I sensed that Michael felt defeated. I asked him about life after death, and what it meant.

His face lit up. He looked around, and whispered, 'I'll tell you later.'

It was safer to discuss religious matters in private, so we went back to his place.

'How does one know for sure there is life after death?'

'Truth needs no arguments to support it,' Michael countered. 'What arguments are supporting the stars in the skies, and where are the proofs for the beauty of your eyes?' He half-smiled, and I could not be sure how serious he was. 'Let me tell you one or two things that will help you meditate about the existence of life after death.

'For example: the human body – to be satisfied it needs only four things: food; warmth in the form of shelter and clothing; rest; and a partner of the opposite sex.

'Look at Krueger, the Swedish billionaire, owner of many of the match factories of the world. He committed suicide out of melancholy. What reason did he have? His body was fully satisfied. On the other hand, martyrs of all creeds die and suffer in prison, deprived of all these things, and they rejoice. There exists in us something which can rejoice even when the body suffers, and which can be sad even when the body is satisfied:

it is called the 'soul'. Nobody has ever seen a soul. A soul is so independent from the body that it can decide to kill the body for purely psychological motives.

'Like two travellers, the soul and body are walking in opposite directions. The body stumbles downhill: the older it gets the more it decays. The spirit walks uphill, generally becoming more experienced and wiser with age. When the body arrives at the bottom of the hill, which means physiological death, does the soul which has walked in the opposite direction also arrive at the bottom? On the contrary, it reaches the top.'

Just then Michael's mother entered. She inquired about my family and studies, but I am afraid I answered rather abstractedly. I was still pondering on that entirely different world to which Michael seemed to belong.

As he walked me home, he told me:

'I've just remembered an interesting argument that Luther, the reformer, presented for life after death. Suppose we could communicate with an embryo and could tell him about the life a child would lead. He would dismiss our suggestions in scorn. The life in the mother's womb is the only one he knows. But if that embryo could think about his own development, he would say to himself, 'My arms grow. Why? I have nothing to use them for. My legs grow. I have nowhere to stretch. What is the good of having eyes? Darkness reigns. Probably another life will follow this one, in which I will have to run and work, and be able to appreciate colours.' The development of the embryo foretells a future life he has never seen. The same happens to us. We accumulate experience and wisdom, but when we have done so we are ready to play the leading role in a funeral service. So why have we accumulated it?'

We were just arriving at my home. 'Too much intellectual stuff in one evening gives me a headache, so save some for another time, please.'

Christ is risen

The Orthodox Easter celebrations gave us this opportunity. On religious holidays we would be called into school and kept there under the pretext of a social gathering, choir practice, or conference to make sure we would not be in church. On such occasions we would invariably sing the International Hymn of the Communists. The refrain is particularly significant:

'Arise, there is no salvation in kings, landlords, and gods.'

Like it or not, we had to be there. And sing.

One tradition, however, was maintained by most of the Christian population in Bucharest: the midnight Resurrection service. On that night the Communists, just like the powers of darkness, were powerless. Every year people would gather on the plaza near Saint Eleftery Orthodox Church from all over the city and its surrounding districts. It was impossible to count the multitude. This is where Michael took me.

It was my first time inside a Christian church. I looked up to the high cupola and saw paintings of an ox, a lion and an eagle. They seemed rather sacrilegious.

'I did not expect such animals to be portrayed in a holy place,' I told Michael.

'Look there at the drawing of Jesus as a shepherd with his sheep,' he replied. 'This is a place which embraces the whole of creation: the saints you see on the pictures there, the angels, the sinners and criminals of all shades in the congregation. I find it only fitting that animals should be here as well. They are God's creatures, too!' He was in a rather romantic mood. Later I learnt that the paintings symbolised the Evangelists.

We filed out with the crowd, every person holding a candle and chanting songs of expectation about the Light to come. An atmosphere of holiness and celebration filled the warm, late spring night. The priests, attired in their most beautiful robes, emerged in procession from the church, raising their hands in blessing as they repeated an old melody similar to our Jewish hymns.

'Christ is risen from the dead,
  Conquering death through death,
  And giving life
  To those who are in the grave.'

They halted, and a priest cried, 'Christ is risen!'

'He is risen indeed!' the whole multitude shouted joyfully in answer. 'He is risen indeed!'

One by one people lit their candles at the flame carried by the priest who had announced this strange news. Then they turned to each other, embracing and kissing. The plaza turned into a sea of flickering lights. It was the first time in my life I had attended such a ceremony, and I was completely puzzled by it. Suddenly I felt Michael putting his arm around my shoulder and kissing me fraternally on the forehead. This, too, was a surprise!

As we moved away I could see tears of joy in people's eyes as they walked away with their candles, still chanting, as if trying to prolong that peaceful, wonderful feeling of the presence of God which had descended upon them. The worshippers walked with an enraptured look on their beaming faces as though touched by God, as though they were already treading on the white carpet of clouds, led by Christ into Paradise for eternity.

For a long time we walked in silence. The stars had never sparkled so brightly for me. 'Heaven is beautiful,' Michael commented. 'It would be a great pity to miss it.'

To my surprise I heard myself asking, 'I wonder how much is essential? Is the whole thing just a highly impressive show, or do you believe too that Christ rose from the dead?'

'Yes, you are right to wonder,' Michael replied. 'This is the proper attitude before a mystery. Did the resurrection really happen?'

'Let's start with the fact that Christ was really dead. Not only did he die nailed on a Cross, but he had his heart pierced with a spear after his death. Afterwards the corpse was put in a tomb, which was then sealed.' Michael was warming to his theme, but suddenly he broke off, and looked cautiously around. There was no-one within earshot. Reassured, he continued,

'Now, how did the resurrection happen? The disciples have left it in writing that they met him after his apparent death, and spoke and ate with him. The fact is that the tomb was empty by Sunday morning. Later, one of his apostles would stand in a market-place a few hundred yards away from the tomb and proclaim that Jesus was alive. He could easily have been laughed to silence by his adversaries, had they been able to produce the corpse, but it was not there.

'If no miracle of resurrection happened, what is the alternative? That the disciples stole the corpse, shall we say, for a more decent burial? I have learnt to know men. My father was one of the most beloved preachers in Romania. When he was arrested, his admirers did not rush onto the streets to demonstrate. He had high connections abroad. They did not intervene to save him. The apostles were cowards too, they wouldn't have risked their lives for this. Some suggested that Jesus swooned – quite a swoon, since his heart had been pierced – that he came back to himself in the cool of the tomb and returned to the disciples. Yet surely a naked weakling who crawled back to them could not have possibly impressed them as a conquering Saviour as Christ did, so much so that many were to die for their faith in him.

'Could a hallucination have revolutionised the world and given rise to the Christian civilisation? I need no argument for myself that Christ is alive: I have met him. I have met you too, and I don't need any proof of that.' We stopped at my door.

He added, 'When you discover God, you will need no proof. It will just happen. He is everywhere. One day you will simply become aware of this.'

CHAPTER FIVE

Last days in 'Paradise'

Joanna was free.

Joanna was my desk-mate. When she burst excitedly into class one day, eyes shining, gasping 'He did it! He did it!' we all knew this was some kind of happy ending for her.

Joanna's father used to have a well-paid, very secret position. He would stay away from home for weeks, returning with beautiful presents obviously from abroad. Then he would lock himself in his room for days and get drunk.

On one occasion, more drunk than usual, he tearfully confessed to his wife and daughter that he had been a driver for Romanian Intelligence in Western Europe. His job was 'accidentally' to run over persons opposing the Romanian government, or spies no longer of use. Now, suddenly dismissed as 'unreliable', he knew what awaited him. He was right: soon he was found dead – in prison, under 'mysterious circumstances'.

Joanna's mother met a French doctor at an international medical congress in Bucharest. He fell in love with her, and yearned to take her and Joanna to Paris. He would send them clothing, fountain-pens, key-holders, nylons, which were unimaginable treasures by Romanian standards. Joanna would report every detail to me. Now she triumphantly announced that the doctor had received permission from the Romanian government to marry her mother. It was an involved project, with heavy bribes every step along the way, but it worked, and Joanna soon left the country.

On my way home from school, I used to day-dream I was in Paris with her, window-shopping on the Champs-Elysées, or sitting in a famous café with young Frenchmen, sipping espresso coffee . . .

From one of these day-dreams I awoke, bumping into Michael, who asked me to meet a friend of his on Saturday night. It did not seem a glittering alternative to coffee in the French capital, but I accepted.

Eugene, his friend, was a shy and soft-spoken individual. He invited us to a 'House of Culture' – a neighbourhood club which was naturally under the Party's close supervision.

Every activity glorified the Party in some way, including the chess, drama-circle and choir. Even the dance-music was interspersed with Party marches. However, Eugene was quite interesting and the three of us enjoyed ourselves talking.

After a while, a stranger asked me to dance with him. I politely refused since I was in the middle of a conversation.

As we were ready to leave, another man tapped me on the shoulder, saying, 'The director wants to see you.'

That sounded like an arrest. He led the way down a dingy back staircase, Michael and Eugene following me, to a room below street level where two men sat playing chess. One was the man I had refused to dance with. Though they protested, Michael and Eugene were told to wait outside.

Still playing chess, my would-be dancing-partner questioned me laconically about my school, my teachers, and the two men with me. At that point I was not only scared but also boiling with concealed indignation at the questions, and at his manner. I gave the information about my school but said as little as possible about my friends. Why was I subjected to this interrogation? Had I done something wrong?

'Of course,' came the rude reply. 'Why is your dress so short?'

This was too much! When we entered I had noticed a young woman in a tight skirt above her knees, plus a tight décolleté sweater. My dress, pink and childish, covered half my knees – yet Comrade Cleavage had not been interrogated about her 'anti-Party' party-dress.

Obviously, this official, whom I had rejected, was seeking to harrass me and my companions, and my dress was only a pretext. As a Party representative, he could file reports which would get me thrown out of school, and Eugene out of university.

But Michael's position was the most perilous. Had my interrogator found out that Michael's father was in jail for religious 'offences', he would have leapt at the chance to lift this incident out of the report-to-your-school category and onto the front pages. Then he would really be a hero to his Party superiors for providing them with ideal anti-religious news. I could already imagine the headlines:

JAILBIRD PASTOR'S SON CORRUPTS SCHOOLGIRL NEIGHBOURHOOD CLUB SHOCKED BY IMMORAL DRESS AND BEHAVIOUR

What a gift this would be to the Party propagandists! And how swiftly it might lead Michael to jail.

I was truly scared by the time Michael and Eugene were called back in for questioning. My insistent inquisitor had soon been grilling us for more than an hour. At last I interrupted.

'Look, if you have something against me, if my dress is too short, you know my school. Report me, I will answer for myself. And now, do you want me to ask forgiveness? All right. I am very sorry. *Please* forgive us. *Please* let us go now.'

He looked triumphantly at his colleague, then turned and frowned at us.

'I will let you go, but I'm also going to report you to your teachers.'

As we walked to the tram we did not feel like starting a conversation. We were all badly shaken, feeling horribly debased and powerless. Once in the tram, however, Michael mustered his usual optimism and smilingly whispered, 'It's good to be free! Thank God!'

Two days later, my head teacher read me the report. I could not believe my ears. Two pages of comments on my dress!

I simply said: 'In my opinion it was not too short, but I will bring it to school tomorrow and let you judge.'

My logic got me into trouble again. I wasn't supposed to defend myself, or argue the point. When the Party speaks, an accusation means guilt. The teacher insisted that I bring one of my parents, and confess.

My dear parents had enough problems already. The president of the boot-repairing co-operative was envious of my father's skill and success, and threw him out. Father was therefore desperately trying to convince another co-operative of his talents and so create a new job for himself. My father fits exactly the Talmudic expression 'The man who does not rely on fortune

68

postpones misfortune.' My father did not wait for 'luck', but tackled things himself. A Jewish rabbinical book explains why the Israelites are compared to a dove: all other birds rest when they are tired. Not so the dove. Even when tired it flies with one wing while resting the other. This is how my father was, and still is.

I felt terribly ashamed at having to trouble him with such stupidity, but I had no choice. At school, he was subjected to an hour of reproaches from my teacher. Then I had to confess my 'guilt' and promise never to do it again – never to do what?

After that, I felt very insecure. I was shocked to realise I was becoming the end-product of what Communism strives to create: insecure people, always afraid of being accused of wrongdoing. As I left school that day I felt so resentful and bitter that I indulged myself, inwardly, in cursing it. Let it burn down!

Next day, as usual, Clara and I met on the way to school, and I told her the latest news I had received from Bruno. The family had arrived safely in Israel and had been assigned a little apartment in Upper Nazareth. Bruno had a job in a textile factory, and was earning the equivalent of about 100 lei a day, a terrific salary.

We were still mulling over this news when we arrived at school and stopped, amazed. The second floor was almost completely gutted, heavy smoke still billowing out. Students were not allowed to enter. Militia, firemen and other officials swarmed everywhere.

Soon the head teacher appeared and sent us all back home. Deep inside, I was happy. The burning of the school gave me a tremendous, though scary, satisfaction. To my childish mind this was exactly what it deserved, and having one's angry prayer answered so promptly in this way, I had to admit, was a lot more exciting than finding a pair of mislaid socks!

When we heard the true story of the fire, I felt utterly miserable. I certainly did not want my curse on the school to come true in the way it did. It seemed that it was not an accidental blaze, but had been started by several boys, aged twelve and thirteen. Despite their youth they were imprisoned for up to six years. All, of course, were routinely and most severely beaten. Some went into solitary confinement and starved for many days in water-logged cells.

The leader of the group was the son of an intellectual who had been imprisoned by the Communists for agitating against the Party. Deprived of his father and struggling hard for survival, the son had become so desperate that his only thought was for revenge.

When I arrived home I found mother crying. She was unable to speak, gazing at a postcard. I took it from her. It was from the Ministry of the Exterior: obviously it had something to do with our application, processed months before, to leave for Israel. Here, at last, was the answer: the word 'positive' was encircled.

Mother, I realised, was crying out of sheer relief – and probably also because she knew what turmoils and tensions lay ahead before we could actually leave. But I was overjoyed and started leaping around the house.

Thirty days to freedom

First my parents had to present this card to the central militia headquarters, where they were told to get out of Romania in thirty days. Since only their names appeared on the postcard, (my younger sister as a minor was included with my mother) my father asked, 'What about our older daughter?'

The approval should have named us separately. The clerk looked, and found no approval on my file.

'I don't have time for you,' he muttered. 'You go ahead, and your daughter will follow when she receives her approval.'

Father was shocked.

'Would you abandon your sixteen-year-old girl alone in another country, not knowing if she will ever be allowed to leave, with no means of supporting herself, and forbidden to work before she is eighteen?' He was quite adamant. 'No, we couldn't possibly do that. If we can't leave together, none of us will leave!'

The clerk took the files back, refusing to indicate how long we might have to wait. It could easily mean another fifteen years. Mother and father came home crushed.

As time passed we naturally grew more and more anxious to know if any progress was being made on our papers. There was one possible way of finding out: from the Israeli Consulate in Bucharest. This was very dangerous, because anyone going there was followed by the police, usually sacked from his job, or at least beaten up. Father decided it was worth the risk.

My friend Clara and I were waiting for him at home. Three hours elapsed. Worried, we set out for the Consulate to meet him. Through a window, we could see there were only three people in front of father, so we quickly left. He would have been upset to know that we had even set foot near the place.

We thought we were being clever. We kept looking back to see if anyone was following us; no, we could not spot anybody. We walked around town, stopped in front of a record shop, listened to the music for quite a while before taking a tram to a nearby park and wandering across it. Only after that did we start back for home.

When we arrived, father had still not returned. However, our house manager and a secret police officer were there. Like every house with more than two families, ours had a manager. He was directly responsible to the neighbourhood militia for the number of people who lived in the house, and had to report any visitors who stayed overnight. The officer went straight to Clara, and asked her name.

He looked in the register.

'You're not listed. What are you doing here?'

'Just visiting,' she said.

'Show me your identity card.'

'But I don't have it with me. I can go home and get it. I don't live far.'

'How long are you planning to stay here?'

'Maybe an hour or so,' she said. I tried to straighten the situation by vouching for my good friend, but the officer insisted on questioning her to make sure she was not from another city. After that he looked around, then dismissed the house manager, and asked me to show him the whole apartment.

I did. His official tone disappeared as he whispered:

'Look, I know you went to the Israeli Consulate because you want to leave the country. I want your apartment. In return I will try to arrange for your family to receive their exit visas. Just tell your parents that. I shall be in touch.'

With this he left. Clara and I were shaken up. We did not

know whether to believe him or not. We realised we must have been followed after all – not just by one but by different people who gave clues to each other. I didn't dare pass on the message to my parents.

Not long after this, however, we received another postcard. We clustered to read it: we were *all* allowed to leave the country! My sister and I hugged father, and mother burst into tears again.

We immediately started making plans on what to sell, what to take, where to obtain the final affidavits releasing us from all obligations towards the different government agencies.

The last day of school arrived. Our head teacher wished us a good vacation, and then told us that the Party needed our help for the next ten days. We were to come in every day to help, voluntarily of course, to restore our burnt-out school.

This cut deeply into the time available for helping my parents with the same tortuous preparations for departure that Bruno had had to go through. But volunteer work must be done. Any lessening of zeal on my part, up to the last moment, could have jeopardised our hard-won escape.

The days flew past. Soon we had all the required papers. All seemed to be going as well as could be expected. The man who was taking our apartment promised to buy everything in it. Yet, he did not pay what was already due on part of our belongings. We realised he was stalling to take advantage of the situation mercilessly, so that at the last moment he would get everything for a fraction of the true price.

Being in the secret police he could get away with it. To my astonishment, when he came to take everything over, it was the very same officer who appeared with our house manager after I had visited the Israeli Consulate. Evidently he had really been able to get our permission through.

We were next called to the Central Militia Headquarters. Our travel certificates were ready if we:

1. Agreed to pay the equivalent of £2,000 (i.e. £500 each) for the 'processing' of our renunciation of Romanian citizenship.

2. Signed documents stating we would not talk against the Romanian government when abroad, and thanking it for allowing us to leave.

3. And just one more 'formality' – the equivalent of £150 each,

for the three of us over the age of fourteen, for the certificates themselves. All monies to be paid within five days.

We agreed and signed.

The squeeze-'em-dry-emotionally-and-financially routine was now at full, agonising stretch, and the man taking over our apartment did nothing to ease it.

He moved in days before we left, to make sure no-one else did. He, his wife and child made themselves completely at home, even helping themselves to the food *we* bought. He also kept eagle-eyed track of what furniture we sold and what we did not.

Now that we unexpectedly and urgently needed the additional £2,600, we pleaded with him either to pay us now or let us sell our belongings elsewhere. He gave us part of the money but postponed the rest. In a nightmare of deception and tension, we had to sneak out some pieces of our own furniture to people who would give us cash on the spot – and risk his powerful displeasure.

We completed all the papers, all the payments, all the train reservations, still afraid that everything could nevertheless collapse about us.

We had 400 lei left – enough to buy four lunches!

A farewell, souvenir photo was taken of Michael, Eugene and me, looking mournful. I still treasure it. Next day they came with us to the train station.

They were the only ones to see us off. Michael's last words were:

'You're going to a country where the supernatural became natural. The Bible says that God dwells there, in Zion, a mountain near Jerusalem. It may sound strange, but this is God's address. I hope you will visit him.'

I was fine until the train moved; then all the joy of my escaping was marred. It occurred to me that we might never see each other again, and I realised how much his friendship meant to me. As the train gathered speed, I felt that a part of me was left behind, and the wrench hurt.

Late that afternoon we arrived at the Hungarian border. The Romanian border-guards searched our compartment thoroughly, making sure we were not taking out any valuables. I wore a ring my grandmother had left me when *she* fled Romania, twelve years before. Mother wore a stone in a simple setting in addition to her wedding ring.

73

The guards took them.

We did not argue. We wanted to get to Vienna, not into a Romanian prison – and they knew it. The guards left. Then, one came back.

'Pull up your skirt,' he ordered me.

Unbelieving, shocked, I asked, 'But why?'

'I forgot to search you.'

'I have nothing hidden,' I said,

'I have to see,' he insisted.

I was shaking with rage, my father, mother and sister were speechless, all of us knowing that this last vulgar indignity was inescapable – and filthily typical.

In the longest and most humiliating moment of my life, he pulled up my clothing and touched me. Then he jeered and left. This is my final, fitting memory of the Romanian 'paradise'.

I cried – and I hope some of my shamed tears were for that sad and twisted man, so debased by the vile system he served.

Early next morning we arrived in Budapest and changed trains. The Hungarians were as badly dressed as we were. Their faces still bore the marks of the horrors they had witnessed when the Russians crushed their uprising in 1956.

When at last we arrived on Austrian soil, how our spirits soared. At once, the houses looked gayer, the grass greener, the trees taller. Even the sun seemed brighter! Maybe it was only in my heart – but I could hear music.

Only those who have crossed literally from one world to another – from Communism to the West – know the unique, joyous lilt of that melody which can never be silenced.

It is the song of freedom.

CHAPTER SIX

Finally . . . a normal adolescence

Two of the most precious words in any language are freedom and faith, two ingredients so very necessary for human happiness.

Under the Communists, the much-trumpeted 'dictatorship of the proletariat' does not even attempt to operate for the happiness of its people. It has been sixty years since the Russians set out to achieve Utopia, without religion, without God; thirty since the Chinese did the same. Why haven't they succeeded?

The answer lies in an illuminating sentence from George Orwell's *1984*, uttered by a blunt spokesman for Big Brother: 'We did not create the power to protect the revolution: *we made the revolution to get the power.*'

That is it. Power itself, over millions of people, is the objective. The Communists have elevated oppression and tyranny to an all-embracing way of life.

In Vienna, we were met by two young Israelis, and spent the night in a huge old building like an army barracks, dating from the time of the Emperor Franz Joseph.

Next day, one of the men took me for a walk along the Danube. While absorbing the river's ageless beauty, I heard from him the harsh facts on contemporary emigration. I did not know till then that Israel, from its slender and strained resources, had to pay about £1,250 to the Romanian government for every Jewish family allowed to leave – and today this figure would be a bargain. Inflation, it seems, has also hit the trade in human happiness, and prices nowadays range on up to £5,000. A sharp rise, literally, in the 'cost of living'.

The following day was my sister's twelfth birthday. We were all discussing what to do with our suddenly worthwhile and promising lives when we were told that seats were available for us, right that very day, on a plane bound for Israel. My

75

sister thus had her birthday party high above the Mediterranean Sea, on our way to the Holy land.

Everything was happening so fast and so wonderfully!

We spent the first hours in Israel receiving our identity cards. What a difference from Romania's endless, cold processing! Not that the busy officials at Lod airport were all smiles and sentiment – life is tough in Israel and this is reflected in the people and their behaviour – but there was a genuine feeling of welcome, of being wanted as a part of a forward-looking, proud and achieving country. 'Shalom' began to ring constantly in our ears, the Hebrew for 'Peace', Israel's universal greeting and goodbye.

My uncle came to fetch us and we went to settle in Nazareth. An agreeable surprise awaited us; we managed to rent a flat opposite my childhood sweetheart, Bruno and his family!

The following months were filled with the excitement of being in an environment totally different from everything I had ever known. There were difficulties and not everyone we encountered was pleasant and generous: Israelis are people just like any other, in infinite variety. But fear had left our lives, and we felt we could stand upright and express our personal opinion on any subject under the sun. We could tell jokes about everything, government included, without risking a spell in jail. This blessing of dignity and self-respect was a constant and priceless joy. It seemed like a dream to us which started in our unbelievably luxurious apartment: two bedrooms, living-room, kitchen and bathroom!

Michael's words about the supernatural seemed religious fancy. Who had time for it?

Father got a job as a specialist weaver in the factory where Bruno worked, my sister and I took a crash course in Hebrew, to prepare for school; and every one of us indulged in . . . eating. We revelled in milk, white bread, butter, and macaroni with cheese. In a few weeks, I went from 95 lbs to 115 lbs.

Eight months later, the weaving factory went out of business and father found work in the southern desert city of Asdod, a good six hours' drive from Nazareth. When the school term ended I went to Tel Aviv for the summer, to live with my aunt and uncle and work in a small shop as a sales-girl. My mother and sister soon decided to join me in Tel Aviv. Naturally, even in one of the world's most crowded cities our dear veteran house-hunter succeeded in tracking down an apartment. Once more our family was reunited under one roof.

The man from Milan

One by one the girls around me were getting married. My friend Clara had recently arrived in Israel. I introduced her to my group of friends. She too, got married.

I did not feel that this was what I wanted, just then. I did not know what to do with my life and grew restless. Bruno and I had drifted apart months ago. Every so often I thought of Michael and, strangely, during those reveries, something of what he said about Christ and eternal life would come back to me like a distant echo and soon fade out again. I would also remember the Easter service at Eleftery Church, the people's faces as though touched by heavenly grace. These were fleeting impressions, yet I now see how I was providentially led toward the decisive turning point in my life.

My father finally found work in Tel Aviv, preparing the basic threads for weaving materials. This is a well-paid specialist job, but, unfortunately, not permanent. He was only employed sporadically, so I had to look for full-time work to help the family's finances.

On the ground floor of the building where we lived, there was a small company which manufactured electrical switches. I applied there and was accepted.

One of the ladies working there, Mrs Buganov, a woman of Romanian origin, soon invited me to meet a distant relative of hers. Let me call him Mr Goldini. He was a millionaire visiting from Italy, looking for an Israeli girl to marry. This invitation sounded like the chance of my life and it could not have come at a better time. My parents were thrilled.

I immediately made up a fantasy as young girls will, – to marry a millionaire, that was what I wanted, and the very reason I had been feeling so restless and unfocussed lately! I imagined what life would be like as a millionaire's young bride in romantic Italy, the land of wine and tenors, of photo-

graphers chasing Elizabeth Taylor (and, of course, me). Mr
Goldini I pictured, naturally, as Vittorio de Sica: older than
me, certainly, but so distinguished, so experienced, so attractive –
in short, irresistible and breathtaking.

Mrs Buganov and I met him in the restaurant of Tel Aviv's
most elegant hotel. He proved to be a short man, in his early
fifties, with lumpy hairy hands, a disagreeable smell about him,
and, should my story ever be filmed, I should warn Signor de
Sica not to expect to play the role: he would be quite unsuitable!

Mr Goldini was born in Chernowitz, Northern Romania,
where my mother was raised. We spoke in Romanian and
German, but in any language the conversation would have been
uninteresting and forced. Mr Goldini prattled about his home in
Milan, his factory, and his holiday in Israel. He didn't really
listen to anything I had to say, so I finally let him talk all the
time and just said 'Yes' and 'No' here and there.

This meal could have been my first gourmet experience,
but everything tasted like dust. All I could think of was: 'Ten
years older than my father. This man, who may want to marry
me, is *ten years older than my father!*'

May want to? After dinner Mr Goldini asked to see my parents
the next evening. Dazed, I mumbled my agreement, feebly.

Mr Goldini arrived punctually at our apartment with an
enormous box of fine chocolates. My mother was charming to
him, and they talked eagerly about their home town. My father
found him enchanting, and wanted to hear everything about the
factory and house in Milan. He acted as if they were already
relatives.

I was in a sorry confusion as I watched and listened. My
feelings were totally contradictory, my thoughts and desires
veering hysterically from one extreme to the other. One moment,
I was intoxicated with the thought of being rich, spoiled, and
travelling in luxury: the next, nauseated at marrying a man so
much older than me, whom I didn't love, whom I didn't even
like: whom, by now, I could not even stand!

I knew that such a marriage would transform my parents'
lives financially. Wasn't it my duty to ease their lot? Was Mr
Goldini such a dismal prospect after all? Wasn't I being unfair
to him, making no effort to like him because I was still dreaming
of an idyllic romance in a childish way.

My inner debate was swinging back and forth. At last my parents escorted Mr Goldini to the door, mother ever so charming. As soon as she had closed the door behind him, she turned to me, the hostess-smile wiped from her lips like chalk from a blackboard, and snapped:

'NO!'

My father shot her a look of startled disagreement, wrenched from his dreams of factory-management and cigars.

'Why not?' he gasped.

'There is no way she will marry somebody she doesn't love.'

'How do you know she doesn't love him?'

'*Look* at her!'

Father at once cut in, intoning a Romanian proverb:

'It is better to be one day an eagle than a whole life a crow.'

'Our daughter is a girl, not a bird,' replied my mother, impatiently.

It broke my heart to hear them arguing.

'But . . .' began my father.

'I will not let her do it!' Then, to me, again, in case I had missed the point: 'I will *not* let you do it, you hear? We will work harder than ever – we will be poor – maybe poorer than we have ever been – '

'Is that possible?' groaned my father.

'. . . but I am not going to sell my daughter!'

I started sobbing, and insisted that something had to be done. We could not go on like this. We could not even afford secondary schooling for my sister.

For at least an hour after I had collapsed, exhausted, into bed, I heard my parents still arguing over the matter. I jammed the pillow over my ears to smother the sound of their conflict. In my innermost heart I did not blame them, nor Mr Goldini for this unlovely situation. I saw that *I* was to blame for allowing the temptation of luxury to mislead me, even for one second. Ashamed, I vowed before I fell asleep, that I would make my parents proud of me. I was going to 'make something' of myself.

Now, with the perspective of time, I understand better what happened. I had seen the thirty pieces of silver, and was tempted to sell my freedom of choice and my chance of love. That I did not is another proof of divine intervention in my life.

Once upon a bus

The first thing I changed was my name. Instead of Frida I chose 'Judith,' which means 'Jewish girl' in Hebrew. It is also the name of the central character in the apocryphal book which bears her name. When the Jewish city of Betuliah was assailed, it was Judith who saved it: she ensnared the enemy's captain, Holofern, by a clever ruse and cut off his head, thus leaving the enemy army in disarray. Judith's unusual bravery made the rabbis exclude her story from the biblical canon. They feared that an attitude willed by God for an exceptional person, in specific circumstances, might serve as an excuse for sinners to make light of God's commandments.

But I did not give much thought to the story when I chose the name Judith. The choice was made by the Frida who once had proclaimed in a Communist school 'I am Jewish and proud of it'.

My melancholy and restlessness were at once replaced by a strange and exciting sense of anticipation. I did not know when something really important was going to happen to me: I just knew it would.

I worked as a secretary by day, and in the evening I studied architectural design. Our family fortunes took an upswing and we were assigned a lovely new apartment in the then growing city of Holon, on the outskirts of Tel Aviv. Of all the moves we made, this was the most exhilarating.

One evening I was travelling by bus to Tel Aviv. I had a date with my group of friends.

Suddenly I recognised two of the other passengers as the Levys, Michael's friends, whom I had once met for a few minutes in Bucharest. I had been keeping in touch with Michael, but not too frequently, because I did not want his secret police file to bulge with letters and photos from Israel.

Finally I plucked up my courage and approached the Levys.

'Do you remember me?' I asked.

They shook their heads, puzzled. 'No.'

'I'm Judith. We met in Michael's home, in Bucharest.'

'Oh . . . wasn't your name Frida?' asked Mrs Levy.

'Yes! But I've changed my name to something more meaningful.'

'You've changed altogether. I remember you as a young girl, but now you are a young lady.'

Three long years had passed since that meeting. I told them some of my adventures and we were stunned to discover that we lived in the same street! They invited me to visit them now that we were neighbours, and we embraced as we parted.

This is not an unusual scene in Israel. People who have not seen each other for years are constantly meeting unexpectedly, delighted and grateful to discover that the other is alive and free. Though meaning can easily be read into the ebb and flow of everyday events, to have bought a flat just across from the Levys, out of three million people, was too much of a coincidence – especially in view of the consequences. In all modesty and gratitude I cannot help but see divine guidance again. This is not an arrogant claim: in fact, though I had set out to become proud of myself, the course of events taught me the value of Christian humility.

I would frequently meet the Levys on our street, but never found time to visit them. I was by now busy working, nevertheless finding time to move around with my youthful friends and attending a stream of parties. At one such party a young man arrived who set everyone's tongue a-buzzing: he was Anton, a well-known cartoonist.

As I needed to write down an address but did not have a pen, I marched up to Anton and asked to borrow his for a few minutes. Surely a cartoonist carried one?

He was amused by my approach, lent me the pen, and asked me to dance when I returned it. That, as they say, was the beginning of a beautiful friendship, and it almost led to much more.

CHAPTER SEVEN

The crucial question

Anton was surrounded by fascinating friends – actors, writers, artists – and through him I met the 'beautiful people' of Tel Aviv. He was delightfully eccentric and creative. At one point he had to do the lay-out for a whole book. He asked me to help him since he was busy with a hundred other matters. I enjoyed every moment of it. At last I thought, I had found *the* man. I liked him, I could share his work, I could understand it.

On my twentieth birthday, he gave me a diamond ring and told my parents he wanted to marry me. He was eight years my senior, mature, and with a terrific career ahead of him. It seemed ideal: there I was, engaged to a celebrity!

We saw a lot of each other, of course, except on one day of the week. On Wednesdays Anton drew his newspaper cartoons, and had to be left in peace. One Wednesday evening, with nothing planned, I went to visit the Levys on a sudden impulse. It was two years since I had met them on the bus, and that evening seemed the right moment to keep my promise.

Their modest apartment emanated peace and contentment. They were not expecting company, but when I arrived they beamed with pleasure.

'We thought you would never come.'

'I like to keep my promises, even this late.'

They gave me the latest news from Michael and his family. His father had been released from prison, but was in imminent danger of re-arrest. Michael had been expelled from civil engineering school – his fourth college endeavour. In a pause in the conversation Mr Levy quietly asked, completely without preamble, 'What is your opinion of Christ?'

It seemed as if he raised this astonishing question simply because it was time to ask me.

'What is your opinion of Christ?' he repeated.

I was caught off balance. I did not want to hear about Christ, in case the knowledge disturbed and upset my present thoughts and beliefs. I was in exactly the same position as Westerners who simply do not want to hear the facts about Communism: they know intuitively that they would find them very hard to swallow, and deliberately prefer the comfort of their illusions, hoping that these will, somehow, defeat the ugly truth. But this is like expecting a wisp of smoke to withstand a hurricane.

Being polite, I mumbled that I didn't know much of Christ but would be 'interested' to hear about him.

This was quite adequate invitation. I learnt, first of all, Christ's genealogy – he was a Jew like myself, born to a Jewish mother, a descendant of King David. From my point of view Jesus could have been a Turk. The important thing was whether he had the answers to questions like 'What is life all about?' Once I began to think, questions crowded into my mind and my former reluctance to learn was shattered. Now it was I who had all the questions.

I had liked Bruno. I was fond of Michael. I had almost become a millionaire's wife. Now I felt attracted to an artist. My father had witnessed many people dying around him, who had also loved and had their adventures. Then came a Hitler, a bomb, or a microbe, and everything was shattered. Or was it? I had been at a church service, celebrating a resurrection. Had Jesus resurrected? If so, did it mean anything to me? Would I die? Should I even consider the matter at my age? Would I, too, rise again? And what about my parents and so many of my family who had died? Was there a God for sure? If there was, why did we have to go through Nazism and Communism?

Why couldn't we find peace even in our own promised land? The Arabs wanted it. They said it was theirs. Was it?

The Levys dealt patiently and wisely with the whirlwind of questions that apparently lay heavy on my heart. It was past eleven when I left. We made plans to meet on Wednesday evenings for a Bible study.

I needed to know the major Biblical prophets for school, so when I came the following week we started with the first book of Samuel. I had never read it before and was very impressed with Hannah. Hannah's husband, Elkanah, had two wives. The other wife had children, while Hannah was barren and very unhappy about it. I immediately identified with her, though her situation was so unlike mine and her story had run its course thousands of years before, in radically different circumstances. Why did her sorrow touch me so deeply? Was it because I, too, felt that to be barren was a painful sin?

A watch needs only one fault to be useless: not to tell time. I had on my conscience sins of disobedience and lust, words spoken to wound; yet what oppressed me far more that evening was that other women bore fruit.

I remembered Michael's mother, so quiet, smiling, understanding, spreading love around her, ready to suffer for her faith. I remembered Judith, whose name I bore; Queen Esther, whom I admired; the many female pioneers who had sacrificed their youth so that the state of Israel could exist. As for me, I could see no fruit whatsoever on my tree: none at all.

I had come to the Levys as a joyous girl expecting a lot of fun from life, but suddenly it seemed Hannah spoke for me when she confessed to the Jewish high priest, Eli: 'I am a woman of sorrowful spirit.' The psalmist says, 'As the hart pants after the water brooks, so pants my soul after thee, my God.' Was I thirsty for God?

Mr Levy was reading Hannah's song after the birth of her first son, Samuel.

> There is none holy as the Lord:
> For there is none beside thee: neither is
> there a rock like our God.

I understood that Hannah had found the Lord, who led her life. He seemed a sure place even during the terrible storms of this world, the blows of which I had felt since my earliest childhood.

> Talk no more so exceedingly proudly:
> let not arrogancy come out of your mouth.

These words seemed singularly appropriate. Humility had never been my strong suit.

The Lord is a God of knowledge and by him
actions are weighed.

To that point I had done whatever passed through my head,
without ever considering that my actions might be judged by a
supreme wisdom. Suddenly I felt as if the Judith who had
arrived at the Levys' only an hour before had melted away
like a snowflake struck by a sunbeam from God. I had been as I
was no more. How could that happen?

Hannah, still speaking to me over a bridge of three thousand
years continued her song undisturbed.

Yes, the Lord kills, but also makes alive . . . he brings
down to the grave, and he brings up. The Lord makes
poor, and makes rich: he brings low and lifts up. He
raises up the poor out of the dust and lifts up the beggar from
the dunghill, to set them among princes, and to make them
inherit the throne of glory: for the pillars of the earth are
the Lord's, and he has set the world upon them. He will
keep the feet of his saints, and the wicked shall be silent in
darkness. For by strength shall no man prevail.

To me it meant that even my conquest of Anton, much
envied by others as it was, could be illusory. I saw myself,
small and insignificant, fighting my way through life like an ant, to
no avail, as long as I tried to run things *my* way instead of
God's.

It was as if, by pure chance, I had found the key to what most
young people consider the mystery of life. Now it was so simple:
God had the key to my soul, and he opened it.

'How come I've never thought about this before?'

'You have to search for "the origin" to find basic truth,'
answered Mr Levy. 'Just as many adopted children spend much
of their adult lives trying to establish who their real parents are
in order to adjust well socially, those who want to "discover
themselves" have to find God who is our origin, our Creator.'

'Yes, but how about those who do not believe in God, or the
Darwinists who believe purely in evolution?'

'It is true even for them,' Mrs Levy answered simply. 'In order

to get their answers they still have to find the origin of the very
first form of life.'

I pursued the point, thinking of Anton:

'How come that, all of a sudden, it has so much meaning to me,
yet if I tried to talk to my friends about God, they would laugh
at me?'

Mr Levy smiled, and turned to his New Testament. 'Listen
to what Peter says:

> Unto you therefore which believe he is precious, but unto
> them which be disobedient, the stone which the builder
> disallowed, the same is made the head of the corner and
> a stone of stumbling and a rock of offence.
>
> (I Peter 2:7, 8)

'But the moment you believe, you join the royal priesthood,
you become holy, you become his,' said Mr Levy.

I remembered the priests covered with the prayer-cloth who
gave the blessing on the great Jewish feast days. What a book
this New Testament must be! You believe in it and become a
royal priest. What could this mean? No king was a priest to my
knowledge, and no priest a king.

'Is that also written in the New Testament?' was my next
question. I did not know what to expect from it, but what followed
was illuminating.

> But ye are a chosen generation, a royal priesthood, a
> holy nation, a peculiar people that he should shew forth the
> praises of him who has called you out of darkness into his
> marvellous light. Which in times past were not a people,
> but are now a people of God: which had not obtained
> mercy, but now have obtained mercy.
>
> (I Peter 2:9, 10)

Mr Levy went on, 'Now this is what the Jewish people are
called for. This is their destiny, but unless they regard God
as their Lord and Saviour, they are like children who, rejecting
their father, remain without protection, without power.'

86

Mr Levy read on to us, from the Gospel according to St Matthew, about the life of Christ and his teaching. Soon it was eleven o'clock again and though I would have stayed the whole night I had to go home.

Back in my bedroom I opened the New Testament at St Matthew's Gospel to make sure that this was exactly what was written.

> At the time Jesus answered and said, 'I thank thee, O father, Lord of heaven and earth, because thou hast hid these things from the wise and prudent, and hast revealed them unto babes.'
>
> (Matt. 11:25)

I continued reading till I reached chapter eighteen, verse three:

> Verily I say unto you, except ye be converted, and become as little children, ye shall not enter into the Kingdom of heaven.

I truly wanted to start all over again, to be like a tiny child, and have another chance. I found myself remembering a lecture I had once attended by a modern psychologist who kept pounding away at the need to change one's life-style.

'Become aware of yourself. Recognise your mistakes. Put them right. Change your life-style! Only so,' he claimed, 'can a person find satisfaction and fulfilment.'

At the time I had not been very impressed, but now it took on new meaning. He had been talking about rebirth – but without knowing the spirit in which it could be achieved.

What modern, God-denying psychologists were recommending as new, ingenious, and mature, was in the New Testament, preached by Jesus himself two thousand years ago. The New Testament had an answer to a very modern problem, the need for peace of mind, satisfaction, and fulfilment.

In order to achieve it I realised that I had to be transformed – to be born again!

A seed of Godhood

Yom Kippur came, the Day of Atonement, on which Jewish people fast and pray for God's forgiveness of their sins during that year. As usual I stayed home and fasted, that year more seriously than ever. Around eleven o'clock in the morning I felt the need to speak to the Levys, to be near them. I found them at home, glad to receive me.

Mr Levy read the ceremonial of atonement as prescribed in the Bible. Two goats had to be brought before the high priest. One was sacrificed to God. On the head of the other, the priest symbolically laid all people's sins and chased it as an act of defiance into the mountains to Azazel – the evil spirit.

'You, the demon who made Israel sin, here take every sin back. They will burden you. Israel is forgiven.'

Mrs Levy noticed my paleness.

'Are you fasting?' she asked.

'Yes.'

'So you recognise that you, too, have sinned?'

'Of course I do.'

'But what is this to God if you fast one day, then tomorrow you turn your back on him and do the same things again?'

'Isn't this what everybody does?'

'Only because they don't believe in Christ as Lord and Saviour. Remember what we read the other evening in Samuel? "And Samuel spoke unto all the house of Israel, saying, if ye do return unto the Lord with all your hearts, then put away the strange gods and Ashtaroth from among you, and prepare your hearts unto the Lord, and serve him only: and he will deliver you out of the hand of the Philistines." And what did the people do? They gathered before the Lord, fasted and confessed, "We have sinned against the Lord! And the Lord, seeing their repentance, smote the Philistines." '

Mrs Levy paused for a moment.

'The Lord was faithful, but all you have to do is turn to the next page and see that as soon as they were secure the people of Israel rejected their Lord yet again. Thus is human nature, wicked and ungrateful to its Creator; therefore he has to provide even the atonement. Those whose sins were forgiven, by being born again, have the power to commit no more sins. But if somehow they fall again in sin, Christ is their permanent atonement.'

I looked at her anticipating the next question.

'Do you want this permanent atonement?' she asked me. accepting his sacrifice for all your sins?'

Like a flash went through my mind remorse for my sins, and the words of Solomon, 'For there is no man that sins not.' God knew them all. It would be just 'bad business' not to accept somebody who had given himself for my guilt, when all I had to do was believe. And I believed. I finally uttered:

'Yes, I do want Christ to save me!'

We knelt down right there. I prayed that Christ would assume my sins and would be my Lord and Saviour from that day on.

When we stood up, the three of us embraced. Tears of happiness were running down our cheeks. I was choking with emotion and could not talk at all. Going home, I felt like flying over the scattered stones on the freshly-raked ground.

Once I was in my bedroom, I lay down, trying to collect my thoughts. I do not know if I had a dream or a vision; either way, the memory is vivid to this day, and I will cherish it forever: I saw myself in an endless narrow ravine, between two vertical walls of rock. As I walked, childhood memories surrounded me. I re-lived past quarrels with schoolfriends and teachers, fights with my sister, arguments with mother, confrontations with bosses and boyfriends. They all seemed to talk at once . . . and suddenly big rocks detached themselves from the distant rim and bounced down toward me, converging from left and right. I was about to be crushed by this inescapable, irresistible avalanche. Its enormous dimensions became horrifyingly clear to me, yard by earth-shaking yard, as the rocks pounded and rolled thunderously nearer and nearer.

To run was useless. Further along the rock-besieged ravine I would be in just as much danger. Aghast, I stood frozen still, then I took another fearful look up – and saw Christ in the midst of the bombardment of stones, his arms outstretched, his face brilliant with light, his voice warm and calm.

'Don't be afraid,' he called out. 'I am bearing your sins now. Nothing can harm you.'

The rocks kept coming, but they veered off around me, leaving me unscathed. It was as if Christ was my shield. Slowly,

slowly, I was lifted by some invisible force to a high, even plain from where I could see my past and future in his care forever. Then everything disappeared – except the assurance that thanks to him I would never again experience defeat.

I understood the dream to mean that life is like a deep and narrow canyon, between two tall mountains, birth and death, where problems fall on us like heavy stones. How precious then becomes Christ, the shield, the Saviour, the only one who can lift us out on the other side of the canyon!

Suddenly it was no longer painful to look back on my early years. One by one memories of childhood came back to me, warm and clear. I was no longer bitter; they were not 'heavy stones'; they became light, and now I could carry them easily. In every stumbling block I recognised the divine hand, guiding my steps, bringing me out of the rough and dark into the light, on the highway that leads to eternal life in Christ.

I realised that I had finished once and for all with 'Frida'. I reached for my diary to record this passage into a new life. This is what I wrote:

> In every mortal body
> Thou hast put, besides despair of sin
> A SEED OF GODHOOD
> So that every time we miss thy way, or fall
> We may still have within
> A CHANCE FOR SAINTHOOD.

For days I did not contact Anton because I simply did not know how to tell him what had happened. I knew that God meant nothing to him, and if I were to tell him that I now believed in Christ as my Saviour he would have thought me crazy. I was not a knowledgeable Christian with every argument, intellectual and emotional, ready at my fingertips: It was all new to me, and though it was cowardly, I just decided not to see Anton then. Let him believe what he wanted!

It was only some time later that I felt strong enough to tell him that my new faith made our relationship impossible. He remained for me a brilliantly gifted man whom I would affectionately remember, but we now lived in different worlds and I could not tear myself in two and inhabit both. No-one can.

While I was breaking away from Anton, I also withdrew from my circle of friends. I knew I would miss them all, but granted a glimpse of my true destiny I also knew that their casual, frivolous ways, though harmless and great fun, were just not for me any more.

I confided in the Levys, who advised me to think over the break with Anton. They were concerned my parents would be angry that because of their influence I had lost an opportunity to marry well, but I accepted full responsibility in the matter.

That evening Mr Levy read to me from Matthew 19:29:

> And everyone that hath forsaken houses, or brethren, or sisters, or father, or mother, or wife, or children, or lands, for my name's sake shall receive an hundredfold, and shall inherit everlasting life.

That said it all. I had no more doubts about this decision.

The sowers

I grew to love and respect the Levys even more as I came to know them better. Thirty-five years ago Mrs Levy had been the young bride of a famous doctor in Romania, Dr King. He took a special interest in the field of hypnotism and became a most sought-after speaker on the subject.

A daughter was born. She grew up into a bright and talented child. She was barely fifteen when, under the Nazi influence, persecution arose against the Jewish population in Romania.

Fearing for her life, as she had been born to a Jewish mother, her father brought her to a young pastor, Richard Wurmbrand, a Jew himself who believed in Christ and led a growing congregation of other Jews who had embraced the Christian faith.

'I would like to have my daughter baptised,' said Dr King.

'Does she believe Christ is her Lord and Saviour?' asked Pastor Wurmbrand.

'What difference does it make? This is not a matter of faith, just to appease those anti-semites.'

The young pastor patiently explained that baptism is a ritual of high value only to the believer, while it meant nothing to Nazi persecutors. To them a Jew was a Jew, regardless of his religious beliefs or affiliations. The Pastor invited the girl to come to church and find out more about the Christian faith. She came several times, then drifted away.

About three years later, one Sunday morning, Pastor Wurmbrand was leaving for church when an inner voice told him to change the subject of his sermon and speak about Christ and hypnotism; yet he knew his congregation would have little interest in such a theme. As he was putting his thoughts together while walking to church, it occurred to him that snakes have no eye-lids. They never blink. When they face an enemy they pierce him with one look, practically hypnotising the victim. This is also the devil's technique: he hypnotises people into thinking that they are doing nothing wrong, only to wake up, too late, to the sad reality of acts committed under the tempter's influence. This is why we need the Lord Jesus, the only one who has power over the devil himself.

One by one Pastor Wurmbrand's parishioners shook his hand with many thankful words after he had delivered this unusual message. The last person was a poised young lady who exclaimed:

'How did you know I was here today?'

'Who are you?' asked Pastor Wurmbrand in return.

'I am Miss King. Remember me?'

Now he understood why he had been troubled in spirit and had had to change his sermon that morning: this girl was providentially there to hear the message of Christ the Saviour in connection with a most familiar subject. She was deeply touched.

The next Sunday she brought her mother along. Mrs King was a dazzling and talented woman, and the two of them soon became most trusted and efficient members of Pastor Wurmbrand's Hebrew Christian congregation. Their beautiful voices delighted the audience with melodies and words composed after their conversion. Mrs King also started visiting women criminals in prison, and through her zeal many prisoners improved and were set free. Prison officials started inviting her and assigning her 'special cases'. That had never been done before.

One evening, during a prayer meeting, a group of about ten young Jews came in to heckle. Pastor Wurmbrand, undisturbed, went on telling the congregation how in times of Roman persecution the Christians had had to live literally underground in catacombs, and were harassed and killed daily. Under these conditions they practised baptism for the dead. Every time a Christian was killed another one stepped forward, took the name of the dead person, and promised to be at least as dedicated as the fallen hero.

'Christ's army must not suffer loss.'

The message was very timely since the Communists were gaining more and more power, and persecution of Christians had already started in Romania.

Not only did the rowdy young Jews become quiet and attentive, they even attended other services. Among them was a fellow who liked to drink and gamble. His name was Levy.

Not long after that, Pastor Wurmbrand disappeared. He was kidnapped from the street and thrown into jail. At the evening meeting, after prayer had been offered for the beloved pastor, young Levy stood up and asked to be baptised. Everybody wondered, but Levy explained that he would like to take Pastor Wurmbrand's place in Christ's army. 'The Church must not suffer loss.'

Years passed. Pastor Wurmbrand was still in prison. Mrs King, now a widow, continued to be very active in the church and helped Mrs Wurmbrand in every way she could. Levy became a preacher, though it was getting more and more dangerous to be a Christian. Levy married Mrs King to give her and her daughter help and protection in these difficult days. The Levy couple became the new dynamo of the Hebrew Christian fellowship formed by Pastor Wurmbrand.

They told me lots of stories about my friend Michael, whom they had known since he was a child who looked up to Mr Levy to fill his father-image. And here I was, too, twenty-five years later, seeing in Mr and Mrs Levy my spiritual parents! I could not stop wondering if I would ever get to meet this Pastor Richard Wurmbrand, who had managed to convey Christ's saving message to a high society lady and a most worldly young man, making them both renounce their previous life and dedicate themselves fully to Christian service. Their shining example was surely responsible for my desire to become a Christian – just as they were!

I asked the Levys to start taking me to regular worship with Jewish Christians in Tel Aviv. The pastor was brother Ostrovsky – a Hebrew Christian born in Russia. He, too, had a story to tell. His father had been killed during one of the pogroms against the Jews. Young Ostrovsky became bitter and full of hatred, but this did not quench the pain of his terrible loss. His soul kept searching for relief.

One Sunday he arrived by chance at a Christian gathering. There, for the first time in his life, he heard a man speaking about loving one's enemies, and how thereby our souls are healed and we may experience joy again. He read a tract and took up studying the New Testament. After meeting others who had been renewed by the love of Christ, Ostrovsky, too, became a Christian.

By an extraordinary chance he and his family escaped from Russia and finally settled in Canada where he started his ministry. Life was comfortable there and he had many opportunities to witness for Christ.

Meanwhile, however, the state of Israel was created. Jews who had fled from Hitler's gas-chambers and furnaces were coming in daily, shocked by the savagery they had been through, and their souls poisoned with hatred. They needed somebody who could remind them of love. These were the people to whom Ostrovsky wanted to minister. He left the comforts of Canada and went to live with the Israeli pioneers, sharing the dangers threatening the new nation. He spread hope and love around him even when rejected.

It was in brother Ostrovsky's little congregation that I first heard people praying for Christian believers in Russia, China, America, and other parts of the world. We also prayed for the Wurmbrands to be released, and for all the believers in Romania, that their suffering be lightened, and the militia's eyes blinded for the sake of those who worship in secret. Yet it seemed hard to believe the Wurmbrands would ever escape from Romania.

At work I was trying to persuade my colleagues to come to

94

the Levys' Bible studies, or the congregation's meetings, but they could not see the meaning I found in Christ. It did not touch them at all. Maybe their insensitivity was due to a traumatic and somewhat natural misconception. Every Jewish family in Israel knew at least one person killed by Hitler, Szalassy, Antonescu or Pavelic – all baptised Christians who boasted of their religion and killed 'in the name of Christ'. I could see no guilt in Jesus just because criminals sought justification in his name. Rebuffed, I simply kept praying that my faith would be strengthened and my life used for his service.

As for my parents, they had hoped at first that my conversion was a fad. Yet there were no unpleasant feelings between us. They let me deal with this on my own.

Two months passed. One day Mrs Levy called me.

'Judith, listen to this! Michael and his parents are in Italy, in Rome! Praise the Lord!'

CHAPTER EIGHT

Changing course

A whirl of questions and conflicting emotions filled my head over the next few days. What was the significance of my friendship with Michael? If God had answered my unbelieving prayers, what else did he have in store for me? If prayer could activate the seemingly impossible, what else should I be praying for? Mercifully, it was not long before I received a letter from Michael. How wonderful it felt to be free, he wrote, reunited with his parents, and pursuing his education in Paris. I wrote back telling him about my new-found faith.

His answer was enigmatic and full of reserve, rather than sharing my enthusiasm:

'God has been present in your life all along, but now you are discovering what you have always been, someone chosen by God. Now you will see God in everything. Don't trouble your soul with questions of religious practice and doctrine, for it knows instinctively the right path, as the compass "knows" how to point North. Your soul communicates continually with the Saviour in silence, without your even being conscious of it.'

At the time I did not understand half of Michael's letter, but I realised I had been nominated to a royal priesthood on the day of my conversion and now I had to be ordained into it – baptism is the ordination of the laity.

On the great day of my baptism, I fasted in readiness for the ceremony which was to take place at dusk. Dr and Mrs Buksbazen, founders and directors of 'Friends of Israel', an American Hebrew Christian outreach organisation based in Collingwood, New Jersey (U.S.A.) were visiting Tel Aviv and someone invited Mrs Buksbazen to attend. As soon as we met, we liked each other. I felt as close to her as to an old friend, but I had no idea that she would treat me, in due course, as generously as her own daughter.

I asked Mr Levy to perform my baptism but out of love and respect he asked brother Ostrovsky to officiate. As we entered the Mediterranean Sea, the congregation on the beach chanted beautifully, worshipping, thanking God.

At the last minute, the Tempter came too.

I was already in the water, when he whispered, 'Have you forgotten the long chain of Jewish martyrs killed by Christians because they clung to the great biblical creed "Shema Israel, Adonai Eloheinu Adonai ehad," – Listen, Israel, our God is the only God –?

I saw before me the thousands of Jews drawn to baptismal fountains under threat of death during the Inquisition era, and the many, many more who in the Middle Ages had slaughtered, with prayers, their children, wives and each other, to prevent them from the 'catastrophe' of being baptised by the Crusaders. The last words of every Jew who died, for what he believed to be the glorification of God, affirmed that God was *one*.

At that moment, an explanation once heard flashed through my mind. Everyone who has a personal experience of God ultimately perceives him as a Trinity: as a Creator and Father, as a Saviour from sin, and as a Presence who works within the heart to make us godlike. Now I knew Hebrew. I knew that 'ehad' in this sentence does not mean absolute oneness – for this the Hebrew word is 'iahid'. 'Ehad' means a complex oneness, as in "Yom ehad', one day, expressing both 'It was evening and it was morning'. Only the complex oneness is referred to as 'ehad'.

The moment brother Ostrovsky said: 'In the name of the Father, the Son, and the Holy Spirit, I baptise you,' I sank into the water. I did it because I was Jewish and I was proud of it. My forefathers, who had suffered at the hands of pseudo-Christian persecutors, were now in another world where this mystery was explained. I felt they would approve of what I was doing.

The sun, like a big red ball aflame, was sinking in the horizon. Coming out of the water I felt like a new person, my spirit was soaring. I fell on my knees, enraptured. I was brought back to reality by the singing of my friends who, one by one, embraced me. Like happy parents at the wedding of a beloved child, the Levys had their eyes full with tears of happiness.

I was almost twenty-one, and it was time for me to become more independent. I found a Home for girls in the centre of Tel Aviv, which offered rooms shared among four girls for a fraction of the going rate in that part of the city. I quickly moved in and made many new friends among the other eighty girls living there.

One evening I was reading my Bible in the common living-room, curled in a corner of the sofa. Soon, after a stream of boy-friends had come to take the girls out, only Giselle, a newcomer from Morocco, and I were left. She sat by me and asked me what I was reading. Though not a believer, Giselle liked to read both the Old and New Testament in French, her native tongue. I suggested we read together in French and translate into Hebrew. This way I helped her learn Hebrew while she helped me with French, and both of us learned from the Word of God. It worked out beautifully.

With Esther, who was aspiring to become a model, I talked about clothing and dance. When we became closer, I attracted her to my little Bible reading corner.

Then there was Hanna, a girl who worked as a secretary and was studying to become a teacher. She talked to no-one. One afternoon I went straight to her and suggested politely the chairs in the room might be put to better use than as paint palettes. She looked at me in amazement, as if asking 'How dare you talk to me?', then she became friendly, acknowledged she was in the wrong, and promised not to do so. I introduced her to the other girls on the floor. For this she was very grateful; she might have lived there another ten years in isolation.

There was also a lady and her niece who had been nicknamed 'the odd couple'. The niece was studying drama and needed to be close to the university. Her aunt, who had never married in order to bring her up, decided to move into the Home and keep an eye on her beautiful niece. The director had made an exception to take both of them in.

The niece was gone most evenings. As I was reading in the living-room, the aunt kept staring at me from a distance. She yearned for someone to talk to. One evening I let her tell me her life-story, and we became friends. Every time her niece acted ungratefully the aunt would retreat to a corner and cry. I tried to explain to her that when you sacrifice yourself for someone, you either do it willingly – without expecting gratitude for it, as Christ had done for us sinners, or you do not do it at all. She recognised that what I said made sense. I also made her realise that only God could reward her for the priceless gift she had given her niece besides her savings: her utter dedication to her.

'Only by staying in the background, helping without mentioning it, will you eventually be thanked by your niece. Constantly begging for recognition may frustrate her to the point of never achieving anything. There would be no future for either of you then!'

She finally understood, but she would still seek refuge in me in her moments of weakness. 'Why aren't you my niece?' she asked bitterly one evening.

'Because if I were, I wouldn't need you, and your life would have no purpose. Be thankful that somebody needs you. That should make your soul happy.'

Other girls told me that even though they could not take the step in faith I took, my newly acquired Christian outlook and willingness to help at least diminished their mistrust of Christianity in general.

I shared all my new experiences with my dear friends, the Levys. One day, Mrs Levy, whom I called illogically, but most affectionately, Aunt Milly, casually asked me, 'How would you like to go to Switzerland to attend a Missionary Bible School?'

Like so many of the most important events in my life, this came most unexpectedly. I was thoroughly startled.

'I'd love to – but I don't have the money to – '

'No problem!'

Mrs Buksbazen, who had attended my baptism, had offered to provide the air-fare, and at the school I was to work half the day and study half the day instead of paying tuition fees.

When I was able to speak, after nodding my shining-eyed, unbelieving acceptance, it suddenly struck me that Aunt Milly had put the whole wonderful scheme together. I flung my arms around her, 'You are like an angel in my life!'

'No,' she protested, 'just a human being with plenty of shortcomings.' She smiled at me. 'Christians are often far from perfect; sometimes they are even great sinners. Their merit is that they acknowledge it, and repent. One day you will find some fault in us too, but when that happens, turn your eyes to Jesus. He alone is perfect. Don't lose your own faith when you see other Christians faltering, but try to pray them out of any sin which may have ensnared them . . . As for the school in Switzerland, accept it as a gift from the Lord. We have been privileged to be used by God as his instruments.'

I did not tell my parents or my boss about the plans, because jobs were scarce and good bosses even more so. Besides I had the strange feeling that it could not be true. How could such a marvellous adventure happen to me?

I went about obtaining the necessary passport, visa, plane ticket as if they were for someone else. To my surprise, everything fell neatly into place, and three weeks later I was ready to leave. I went to my boss and explained the situation apologetically.

'I can't believe it!' he exploded. 'We like you here, and now you are leaving us. Do you understand what it means? If you quit now, who is going to give you another opportunity? Don't you see that you are cutting the grass from under your own feet?'

I could not help smiling, 'By myself I can do nothing; everything depends on God,' I told him. We parted good friends.

Moving on

Then goodbye to the girls in the Home. That evening we had a family gathering at home. Everybody acted casually, but the next morning at the airport we suddenly all burst into tears. It was as if I were leaving for the moon.

As I stepped onto the plane, for the first time all by myself, my heart was as big as a ladybird, as we say in Romania. The engines started . . . What tremendous power it takes to move an aeroplane. If men could make that aeroplane fly, how much more powerful was my Lord! As we took off I realised that I had left everything I valued behind me, everything but him.

Three hours later we landed in Zurich; from there to Interlaken; and a final bus ride to the top of the Mount of Beatitudes – the Beatenberg – where the Missionary Bible School stood. It was magnificently situated. From any place in the building we could see Mount Jungfrau, so every chance I got I absorbed its peaceful beauty.

The School was run very strictly. We awoke at 5.00 a.m. for an hour's private meditation and prayer. By 6.30 we had gathered in the wood-panelled dining-room for a short Bible study and further prayer. Breakfast was followed by four hours of Bible classes. At 12.00 we had lunch. We prayed and sang before and after meals. Some girls worked in the kitchen, others served, and the boys washed dishes.

I started learning German intensively, and within a week I could communicate. The other students were all giggling at my mistakes, but I kept talking! I had too many stories to tell, and the others were curious to know about Romania, Israel, and about me, the only Jewish convert in the School. I wrote many postcards to friends, giving no address, just 'Switzerland'. One card went to Michael.

It was a time of warm fellowship. I would sit at the same table for a certain period and then change seat in order to get acquainted with as many people as possible. There were Christian girls from all over the world – Canada, Surinam, Holland, Germany, Italy, the USA, besides Switzerland. (I don't know about the boys. We were not encouraged to talk to them!)

One night the School secretary woke me.

'Come downstairs quickly, there's a phone call for you!'

My heart pounded. I imagined a hundred and twenty catastrophes as I hurried down the steps.

'Tell me, Judy, how are you?' asked a man's voice, calmly.

Michael! The last person I expected. I stammered, 'How did you get this phone-number? Even I don't know it! And I didn't even tell you exactly where I was . . .'

'Never mind that. Listen, you'd better come to Paris to see me, because I'm leaving Europe.'

My astonishment increased in direct proportion to his calm.

'Paris?' I almost shrieked. 'How *can* I?'

'Well, you take the train from – '

'I don't *mean* that! I mean, how can I possibly leave in the middle of the school year, and without money, and . . .'

'I'll take care of all that,' he said. 'Meanwhile, just tell me: how are you doing? How are things there?'

In my excitement and confusion, I must have been speaking more loudly than I meant to: dozens of girls and teachers were around me, in nightdresses and dressing-gowns, listening to my incomprehensible Romanian with terrified expressions, ready to extend their sympathy on what they assumed to be a 'sad event'.

I cupped the mouthpiece and held my voice down.

'You've woken the whole school, otherwise everything's fine.'

'Good,' he said cheerfully, entirely unworried. 'You'll hear from me soon. Goodnight!'

Sure enough, I heard. The next day Michael's mother called the director, explaining the situation in German, and asking her to lend me the train fare. They would send it back with me.

The director told me she highly *disapproved* of one of her students travelling alone on trains and buses, especially to Paris.

'What are you doing here, Frau Doktor?' I asked, firmly but respectfully. 'Are you bringing up spoiled schoolgirls, or are you preparing us for the tough life of missionaries in the jungles of Africa and the plains of India? Please let me go – if only to prove that I can survive a journey to France in a comfortable train. If I can't, for sure I wouldn't last five minutes on any mission field.'

I must have struck a nerve. She gazed at me quite blankly, as if astounded that I dared have a different opinion, but she gave me two days off and loaned me the money.

To Paris and love

I was packed only minutes before I had to leave for the station. It was one desperate scurry before I could settle into my seat. The journey was not all that straightforward: at Bern I would have to secure a visa to enter France. My every move had to be registered due to my having an Israeli passport.

It was a cold, rainy, and cheerless October morning in Bern. I rang the doorbell at the French embassy so many times, they must have heard it in Paris. At last the caretaker opened to tell me they were closed for two days – it was some French national holiday. Everyone had gone away. I was so aghast, and persistent, that he asked me in out of the rain. He called several numbers, but got no answer. I sat watching, trying to be calm, saying quietly to the Lord, 'If you want me in Paris, please make a way. If not, I will just return, and accept that I was not meant to go.'

Suddenly the front door opened, and a tall, very handsome man came in, shook off a lot of rain, nodded his head to the caretaker and walked on past us. The caretaker stood stunned and open-mouthed. As he came to his senses, he gulped, 'That was the Ambassador!'

By that time, the Ambassador was striding back towards us, smiling and holding an umbrella he apparently had forgotten in his office.

I jumped to my feet, and in one breath and broken French, held together with German and English words, I pleaded for my visa.

'Oh, that's no problem.'

He asked the caretaker to call his secretary, gave him a private number, and said to me, 'She will do it for you.' He put on his hat and left with a smile.

The caretaker phoned the secretary. She would need two hours to get here because she lived quite far out of the city.

I took out my Bible and let the pages fall open at random. I read:

> Lord God of Israel, there is no God like thee, in Heaven above or on earth beneath, who keepest covenant and mercy with thy servants that walk before thee with all their hearts.
>
> (1 Kings 8:23)

To me this meant a 'Yes' from the Lord. The secretary would certainly get here in time for me to be 'visa'd' and on the Paris train at 4.00 p.m.

To save time, I went and bought my ticket, pacing quickly through the hard rain. Then, back to the Embassy. No secretary yet.

An endless half-hour passed before she arrived, looking like an enraged lioness. Obviously she was furious about her disturbed vacation. She threw me a killing look, but issued my visa. It took exactly five seconds to stamp it in my passport. I rushed back to the station. Exhausted, drenched, but victorious, I climbed onto the train, in a compartment with five unknown men. I was certainly glad Frau Doktor knew nothing about this!

It was still dark and cold when I arrived in Paris, early the next morning. I waited a few minutes but could not see Michael anywhere. The station was huge and forbidding.

I phoned him. In a hoarse voice he reported, 'I couldn't come. I'm in bed with a terrible bout of flu. I'm so sorry.'

I am afraid I was not immediately sympathetic. A fight with my School director, a visa obtained from a raging lioness after ambassadorial intervention, mad scampering through rainswept cities, hours in a train with five snoring men of assorted nationalities – and after all that, my host is not there to meet me because he is filled with flu-germs!

I mumbled something.

'Take a taxi and come here,' he wheezed. 'We'll discuss everything when you arrive.'

'Here' proved to be a huge complex which seemed to me as big as the Kremlin and just as inhospitable and unhelpful. Where should I start looking for Michael's apartment out of the hundreds in this massive building? Fortunately his mother came outside and very sweetly received me in her arms and led the way indoors.

Then came the poignancy and wonder of meeting Michael again after five years. I had before me the same Michael – uncombed, a pullover over his pyjamas, sitting up in bed, unshaven – a big smile shining even through the foul fog of flu.

We said simple, rather silly things.

Michael: 'It's so good to see you.'

Me: 'Likewise, if you didn't have the flu.'

Michael: 'Come closer.'

Me: 'No thanks! If I'd known you were sick, I wouldn't have come at all . . .'

But this was my last moment of exasperation with him. Like an irresistible flood, I sensed with surprise that I was really happy to see him, and that he remained the same warm, engaging, confident Michael.

He told me about their escape from Romania. After a series of hair-raising adventures his father had received a call to minister in Paris. So here they were.

'And what have you done, besides promenading the boulevards and the banks of the Seine?' I asked.

'I got acquainted with my two uncles and aunts, and my three cousins,' he began, then added with mock pride, 'I passed all the exams at the Lutheran Theological Seminary, I presented my bachelor's thesis, and I ate a lot of French pastries with loads of whipped cream, to compensate for the twenty-seven years without goodies.'

'Too bad it doesn't show. You look downright skinny and pale.'

'As a matter of fact, how about a French pastry loaded with whipped cream, right now? Let's go out!'

'But you're sick!'

'I *was* sick, until you arrived. Now I'm fine.'

A few minutes later we were walking hurriedly through the cold on the Boulevard de la Somme to the nearest bus station. I was cuddling Michael's arm to get warm while he, seemingly without noticing, kept explaining details about the buildings we passed.

I could not believe that I was *in Paris with Michael*.

We reached the Champs-Elysées near the Arc-de-Triomphe. Michael took me into a typical Parisian drugstore with a café inside, one of those cozy places where I delighted myself with French pastries and hot chocolate and whipped cream, while Michael had tea and honey.

We could not talk fast enough. There was so much to say.

'You can't imagine how glad I was when I received a letter in Romania from Aunt Milly, telling us that you were going to their home Bible studies. Do you know that all the people who came to our house were praying for you?'

'Yes, I can believe it, because we were praying for you too, every time we were meeting. Michael, your escape gave me tremendous spiritual assurance. It was the first miracle I ever experienced. I could hardly believe my ears – and now I cannot believe my eyes that I'm actually seeing you!'

'Then wouldn't you like to marry me?'

I heard myself answering swiftly 'Of course!' We both roared with laughter in the unimaginable joy of finding each other again, after the tension of the past years. The people sitting around us, whispering romantically, grew uneasy. We hurried out and passed a row of cafés with little round tables and chairs, right on the pavement, enclosed in glass for the winter. People were sipping espresso coffee just as in my day-dreams about Paris.

Unfortunately Michael was suddenly hit by a dizzy spell and I

had to rush him home, straight to bed. He had not really re-
covered. It was just a short-lived spurt of energy.

With a typically Parisian quick change in the weather, the
next morning was mild and calm. The sun was shining brightly
through my window as I awoke to hear Michael, from the next
room, 'Judy, hurry! Get yourself ready. We've got to get your
ticket.'

I did not know what he was talking about, but I hurried out
into the little dining-room. Everything was packed. I gaped.

'My father is in the United States,' said Michael, smiling that
patient smile of his when dealing with people who cannot understand what is simple and logical to him, and so complex and
outrageous to them! 'He's on a speaking-tour, and mother and I
are going to follow him. So we must get you a ticket too.'

By now I was roughly a lap and a half behind him.

'But why?'

'You're coming with us,' he said, as prosaically as if asking me
to sew a button on his shirt.

I squealed, 'To *America?*'

'Didn't I make that clear?' he asked, innocently.

'Not quite,' I gasped. 'I mean – '

'Didn't you say yesterday that you would marry me?'

'Uh – yes – but – well – *Michael*! – I thought that was a *joke!*'

'What made you think that?'

'We laughed, remember?'

'What should we have done – cried?'

'Will you be serious?'

'I am serious. Were you joking?'

'No – no, Michael – but we should wait – we have so much to
think about – '

He walked closer to me. I saw in his eyes the look they had had
that glowing Easter in front of St Eleftery Church. He said,
quietly and very strongly:

'God kept us waiting until we were ready for him. He has done
all the necessary "thinking". It is meant to be. You do want to
marry me, don't you?'

'Oh yes! But, I can't go with you right now!'

He threw up his hands as if I was the most illogical infant
ever to skip about the face of the earth.

'What do you mean, you want to marry by correspondence?'

'Wait a minute! I still have to go back to school to become a missionary.'

'Like St Peter or St Paul?'

'Well, I'm not that ambitious, but I'd like to be a good one.'

'They were among the best. Tell me, which Bible colleges did they go to?'

I felt there was a flaw in this argument, but I was in no state to deal with it. All the female in me wanted to be swept off my feet, and succumb to the sheer romance of it all: to indulge in finding, at last, what I had not found in Mr Goldini. At that moment, the temptation to throw every other consideration aside and fly to America was almost overpowering, but I somehow managed to retain a steady outlook and insisted I had to go back.

'I will finish the quarter, and leave in a civilised manner. I can't just disappear that way.'

I could tell, by his brisk nod and look of love, that Michael respected me for this. 'Bible colleges have their value,' he said, 'though one can be a good missionary without having attended one. Spurgeon was a great preacher, yet he never had any special training. The words "mission" or "missionary" never occur in the Bible. Instead, the Greek word "martyrios" – witness – is used. A witness is in this case one who had a glimpse of the eternal beauty and therefore is ready to die for it.

'As you have had this experience, you have to put it to work, and I promise you one thing, Judy: In our family you will have plenty of opportunity for missionary work.' He paused. 'We are going to help the brethren left behind us, behind the Iron Curtain. What better field of service could you ask for?

'There are many missionaries, but few who actually come from Communist countries and dare speak about the religious persecutions there, and the plain hard fact that Christians need help. Remember when we lived in Romania, how disappointed we were every time some important visitor left – and nothing changed because he didn't tell the truth when he went back to the West?

'Therefore we must take the opposite stand, openly tell the West what is going on in Communist countries and help Christians who are in trouble and need there.'

He paused again, and looked at me warmly smiling:

'So finish school as soon as you can, and come to work!'

Punctuated by a big hug and a kiss, this felt very inviting. It all connected together: what to do with my life, and with what partner. I realised Michael would be indeed the perfect husband for me. He wanted me to help him, he needed me, and he believed I was capable. In fact, with touching frailty, he needed me right there and then, even to carry the light load of his briefcase as we walked to the travel agency. Poor soul, he was exhausted from that terrible flu.

Back in Switzerland, air ticket to the United States safely in my bag, I resumed my study and work. Michael and I had agreed that I should wait till he established himself. Every day, however, I received postcards which grew bigger and bigger. Finally I got one which measured 20 inches by 30 inches saying, 'Now or never! Unless you come by December 1st, forget it!'

I did not forget it. A few days later I started on what seemed an endless journey to New York, the dream of so many generations, and place of so many happy endings.

For us it was a beginning.

CHAPTER NINE

A hurricane called Richard

America the beautiful might be the destination for many people, but to reach it at twenty-two, and in love, was more than I had ever dreamed. Yet here I was. For the last twenty-four hours I had raced in buses, trains, and planes, from Switzerland through Germany, Luxembourg, Iceland. My heart thumped hard as we flew over New York harbour with its majestic hostess, the Statue of Liberty, lighting our way in. I felt again that strong, overwhelming joy that freedom alone can give and that revived me. Not even the visa, vaccinations, and customs formalities at the J.F.K. Airport could dampen that exuberant happiness.

To make it even more unforgettable, here at last, halfway round the world, Michael came to meet me. We embraced and kissed the very second I could step out of that enormous customs room, forgetting that we were in public, as if the whole world around us had faded away.

Soon we were on the way to Manhattan. I should have been completely perplexed by the freeways, the multitude of cars and sky scrapers, yet those vast symbols of civilisation hardly impressed me. My whole attention was taken by the modest wedding ring Michael had set on my finger shortly after I landed. I looked at it as if I had never seen anything more precious or more beautiful.

The other surprise was that Michael had arranged for us to meet his father in Chicago where he was speaking. Only after that would we fly 'home' to California.

We arrived shortly after Pastor Wurmbrand had started his sermon. The church was big, with every modern comfort: beautiful furnishings; amplifier; air conditioning; every person present was superbly dressed. Yet I had little time to observe the surroundings, my attention was caught by the preacher. A

New Zealand reporter once wrote, 'I met a hurricane called Richard,' for he seemed to touch in one way or another every single person in the room. His challenging eyes allowed nobody to lower their own for a second, while his sermon scattered seeds from which the hearers' own thoughts would grow.

He suggested that in New Testament Greek the verb 'genao' means both 'to be conceived' and 'to be born' – two very different matters. 'So the words of the Lord in John 3:3 can truthfully be translated in two ways: "Whoever is not conceived anew cannot see the Kingdom of heaven" and "Whoever is not born anew cannot enter it". 'Many assume that they have been born again, when in reality they have only been conceived again. Your spiritual life is still in embryo, as long as your deeds have not won other souls to Christ.'

Now I could understand something of Michael's thoughts on the difference between a missionary and a witness. This was a witness who was a missionary. For a moment I mused. What if my place in heaven was not so assured, after all?

I had received the simple beliefs of faith from the Levys and I certainly felt born again. Later, as I read the Scriptures more fully, I found out that those who were so sure to be right were often wrong. The people of Jerusalem in the time of Jeremiah had no doubts about their righteousness, yet they went into exile all the same. The Jews in John the Baptist's days were sure of their status as the chosen people, but the axe was laid to the root of the tree. The Pharisee in the parable was self-assured too, whereas the publican was not. I had to ask myself, 'Am I also in the wrong?'

Pastor Wurmbrand was still speaking. 'Never rely on your being born again as a warranty for entering heaven. We are saved not by having repented truly, nor by having become new creatures, neither by being God's children, but solely because of what Christ did for us. It is no achievement of our own.

'Often we come very near: we may be intellectually convinced of the supremacy of Jesus; we may decide to adopt his moral ideals, receive his forgiveness, even accept him as Lord and Saviour, but we are truly in Christ only when he, by the Holy Spirit, runs our lives.

'So, regarding your own state, always fear and tremble, even if the whole world looks up to you as to a saint, but be absolutely confident about the sufficiency of Christ's sacrifice, and the guidance of the Holy Spirit.' That was the very reassurance I needed.

While we looked for a seat Michael caught his father's eye, and pointed to me as if saying, 'Father, meet Judy!' Pastor Wurmbrand immediately reacted with innocent informality.

'My son has just communicated that his bride has arrived. I would like everyone to see her so that I can have a chance to do so too. You see, when I was taken to prison I left behind a boy of nine. When I was released a grown man greeted me. I could hardly believe it was the same little Michael I had longed for in all those years of separation, but it was him all right. A few days ago he told me he would be getting married, and now I am seeing my daughter-in-law for the first time. OK, Michael, I approve!'

This public inspection was thoroughly embarrassing, but I was very moved by the warmth and simplicity of this welcome message. What the pastor added made it even more memorable.

'Far away from my loved ones I used to spend a great deal of time in prayer for them. I prayed especially for Michael, that Christ himself would guide him and protect him from the blows of hostile authorities. I was troubled by one thought in particular: would he remain faithful in spite of growing up without a mother or father, and shunned by his peers?

'The Lord in his mercy took good care of Michael. He was confirmed when his mother, also in prison, in rags and dishevelled, could only whisper to him, "Michael, believe in Jesus, he loves you!"

'God then guided him to study theology. A few years later came the miracle of our being purchased and coming out to the West. Now I prayed for a Christian wife for Michael, and the Lord answered this prayer too. But the unexpected surprise, a delightful bonus, is that Judy is my own spiritual grand-daughter, for she was brought to Christ by my spiritual children, the Levys. This is so much more than I asked for, so my Lord, I thank you yet again! As for you, Judy – God bless you! You are an answer to prayer.'

After the service we had a prolonged lunch. Pastor Wurmbrand asked me many questions, about me, my family, and especially about Israel. I answered as fully as I could. For a while his eyes remained dreamy, then with a spark of joy he asked, 'Would you like to hear some of your husband's "pearls" when he was barely taller than my knee?'

'Please. Did he say something silly for a change?'

'Well, not quite. I found notes I made some twenty-three years ago when he was about four. We were in the middle of the worst period of Nazi persecution. People who came to us were constantly reporting how they had barely escaped being shot or sent to concentration camps, and we were actively engaged in stealing Jewish children from the trains that were taking them to extermination camps. I did not know how long we would be able to pray our way out of Nazi hands, so I decided to prepare Michael for that grim possibility. His first question was:

' "Will they take us by car?"

' "Naturally," I replied. His face lit up.

' "Then at last I'll get a chance to see the town!"

'I insisted, "But you will only get a short ride, after that they may shoot you."

' "And then we will die?" Michael asked.

' "Of course we will die," I answered.

' "Never mind, father, we will first die a little, then we will be with Jesus in heaven and the police will not be able to reach us, because they don't have long enough ladders."

'One day I told him the story of Adam and Eve. He listened solemnly, then thought a moment.

' "If Adam," he concluded, "instead of throwing the whole guilt on Eve, had joined with her against the serpent and repented, God would probably have allowed them to remain in paradise." '

The Pastor was obviously very fond of his son. He smiled at us. 'Just two more. After telling him about the Garden of Eden, I read him the story of Cain and Abel. He mulled it over, then commented, "Abel wasn't a good man either, remember he killed an innocent sheep."

'But repentance seemed the issue he was most concerned about. After I had read him the passage in which God orders Joshua to kill the Canaanite people, Michael exlaimed, "Of course, God ordered that before he became a Christian, so God is forgiven." '

Against Goliath

I was so happy to be in America, a country where every one could breathe and walk freely. Romania had been one big prison. Israel was free, but besieged: Hitler had thrown Jews into burning ovens; now their enemies, lurking all around, made no secret that their purpose was to throw all of Israel into the sea. Only in America could I shed my fear. I was thankful to God and all those who had worked and fought so that such a bastion of freedom could exist.

In comparison with people in Romania and Israel all Americans looked like millionaires. Material richness is a gift from the Creator. Michael and I did not have it, but we rejoiced with those who rejoiced.

Michael's father had the impressive title 'Overseas Director' in an organisation designed to help Christians behind the Iron Curtain. Due to the impetus of his speaking engagements the need for office staff was so great that, the day after our modest marriage service, Michael and I were at work there. The correspondence we had to deal with revealed that all was not complacency and apathy in the West. Out of love towards Christ many Americans are interested in the fate of the persecuted Christians in Communist countries who are ready to suffer for their Saviour. That was very heartening indeed.

As far as the organisation was concerned, it was a complete disappointment and we decided it was better to disengage ourselves.

This was a real trial for my faith. As I look back, I understand how important it is to tell young converts, from the very beginning, about all the dangers and snares of Christian life, and about the problems they may encounter in the Church herself. This experience was even more bitter for my father-in-law, yet he told us to maintain a cheerful perspective.

'As Christ is one person with two natures, human and divine, so the Church has two sides, also human and divine. Whoever has God as his father has the Church as his mother. She has kept the word of God during dark and bloody centuries, giving us the rule by which we can evaluate not only our lives and the world, but the Church herself. She has kept the sacraments. When, after years in prison, I re-entered a church for the first time, I had the feeling the altar was surrounded by angels, whispering their joy to each other at seeing all the souls there.

'The Church is the representative of heaven on earth. In it you are surrounded by the cloud of witnesses who have served faithfully and brought us the burning torch of faith.

'The other side of the Church is made up of humans. But, like a loving mother, the Church keeps sinners at her bosom. Let us not be harsh in judgment, but be wary not to fall into similar traps ourselves.

'I have been imprisoned with thieves and crooks. They told me their life stories, filled with the traumas they had experienced in early childhood.

'Romans 3:3 reads: "All have sinned." I find that very comforting. It means that all those who were around me before I ever sinned were themselves sinners. I have been sinned against before starting to sin myself; I have inherited sin. Christians do not condemn sinners, but pray for them.'

As we were starting our new organisation the Pastor's first book, *Tortured for Christ,* was due for publication. Ten thousand copies had already been printed, but the organisation from which we broke away professed no further interest in the book. The edition came close to being destroyed for lack of funds. We finally worked out an arrangement with the printer whereby we would pay in instalments as the books were sold.

An American lady who had befriended us offered the use of her Christmas mailing list. Michael and I spent days and nights typing labels, and made the first mailing announcing this book. After an inauspicious start it later proved a bestseller in fifty-four languages, and many millions of copies have been sold around the world.

We were consumed by a sense of urgent duty towards our brethren left in Romania. Like David before Goliath we felt small and insignificant, but like David we drew strength and courage from the Lord. Our help meant little, while the needs were overwhelming; we knew that, but we also knew that the Lord expected only our best and that was what we intended to give.

While my parents-in-law globetrotted tirelessly on speaking engagements, Michael and I organised the office-work. Orders started pouring in and we processed them promptly. The ten thousand volumes dwindled rapidly. Many readers learning about today's martyred churches asked if they could be of some help. Soon we were being swamped with letters, and had to move the 'office', which until then had been our kitchen table, into separate quarters.

We published, folded, and stuffed our first newsletters in envelopes, stamped and mailed them. We were, as Americans say, in business – the business of truth and assistance, doing the work we believed we were meant to do: to bring JESUS TO THE COMMUNIST WORLD. The funds needed were slow in coming, but we refused to ask for money. Pastor Wurmbrand taught us how to rely on God for finance, illustrating his point with tales of missionaries from the past. One day he told us about Hunter and Percy Mather, who got lost during a missionary journey in Mongolia while crossing the vast Gobi desert. One evening their servant told them desperately, 'We have only two handfuls of rice and one of lentils. Starvation can only be a few days away.'

'You are wrong,' Mather replied. 'We have only a little bit of rice, a handful of lentils – and God.' He sat down in prayer before his tent and remembered Psalm 23:5 'Thou preparest a table before me . . .'

Soon they were found by the first geographical explorer-caravan to cross the Gobi desert. The British explorer gave them everything they needed, and led them out of the desert to safety.

Like them, we did not worry where funds would come from; we just worked and prayed.

Michael's ordination

July the 1st, 1970, found us in a little village in the Swiss Alps, Château-d'Oex. Travelling with Michael helped me to understand how St Bernard of Clairvaux could ride a whole day along Lake Geneva without even noticing it, while all the Apostle Paul saw of Athens was a city full of idols. The Bible also tells us much about Egypt, yet does not mention the pyramids or the Sphinx. Landscapes and monuments interest Michael very little. One subject alone counts for him: human beings and their soul.

By now our organisation – Jesus to the Communist World – had grown notably. We had branches in every continent. When we went to bed, tired, our Australian, European, African, and Japanese brethren were rising to tackle a new day. We could truly say that the sun never set over our work. Our mission workers from around the world were going to meet here for our mission's first international conference. One of the highlights was to be Michael's ordination as a pastor in the Lutheran Church.

It took place in the tiny village chapel, the setting sun streaming in through the stained-glass windows.

Bishop Monrad Norderval from Norway was officiating. He was assisted by several high dignitaries: Bishop Wesley of the Indian Methodist Church, Pastor Stuart Harris from England, Rev Maris of the Dutch Reformed Church, also General Secretary of the International Council of Christian Churches, Rev Myrus Knutson, of the American Lutheran Church, a very dear friend, and of course Michael's father, Pastor Richard Wurmbrand, all men of high spiritual stature with long years of Christian service behind them.

In his ordination address, Bishop Nordeval told Michael, 'I have ordained you as a pastor, but perhaps also as a future martyr for Christ.'

Michael's reply was simple and direct.

'The Lord urged humanity, "Repent, the kingdom of heaven is near." Compared to what is happening in the world today, the sins of Jesus' contemporaries were small; their worst sins were limited to a national scale. They could not instigate world wars, drop nuclear bombs, dynamite buildings. Neither could they bring crime and immorality into every home through television, or boast to the whole world over the radio. The most renowned writer of poisonous things was not read by more than a thousand people. The Bible says, "Take out the little foxes, that spoil the vine." By comparison it would have been much easier to repent of sins when Jesus walked on earth.

'Mankind has allowed two thousand years to pass without heeding the call of Jesus. What would have been relatively easy then has become very difficult now, but nevertheless *now* is still the appointed time. Tomorrow might be like Noah's last day before the flood.

'Our duty as Christians has become more urgent than ever. The Lord's last command was "Go and teach all nations". When he comes back, his first question will be, "Did you teach all nations?" This means that we must teach men about Jesus not only where it is acceptable and easy, but also in places of desolation and terror, such as the Communist and Moslem worlds.

'I promise, by the grace of God, to dedicate myself to this task.' As his wife I fully assented with him, and felt he had made this pledge on my behalf as well.

Words became deeds as we returned home and the work grew daily. So did the attacks against us. Not only was the Communist press full of wrath, but some Christian Evangelical associations also reproached us, claiming that it was deceitful to smuggle Bibles into Communist countries. We discussed this particular point together. Michael recalled an apocryphal remark of Jesus,

'One day, seeing a man working on the Sabbath, Jesus said to him, "If you realise what you are doing, you are blessed, but if you do not, then you are accursed, and a transgressor of the law." This is the whole spirit of Christ's teaching. If we were smuggling Bibles in order to avoid paying duty or to make a profit, it would be wrong, but since we do it because the Communists forcibly hold one billion people from hearing the saving news of the gospel, then what we do is right.' We ceased to worry about these attacks.

Sometimes I think my part in all this activity is menial, but the Bible has a unique approach to such things. All other chronicles only record the names of kings, generals, and other notables. Without neglecting the kings, the Bible gives long lists of doorkeepers and timbermen who cut wood for the Temple. Even janitors who swept the Temple with a broom are worthy to be remembered, still sacred after thousands of years. This is the only book which values those who performed small and despised jobs out of love for God; for there is also a mystic value in mundane service, no less important than prayer, contemplation and preaching. One of the great mystics, Brother Lawrence, was assigned to sweep a large monastery. One can serve God in any work: writing notes, answering mail, meeting visitors to the mission, answering the phone.

Though involved as I am in the work of the mission, I feel my main task is to provide my husband and our two children with a pleasant home. Our daughter Amy also cooperates in this. If Michael feels tired, and his prayers are shorter than usual, she will not allow it. She plucks him by the sleeve and tells him, 'Daddy, we didn't pray enough.'

On other occasions she will offer her interpretation of Bible stories. It was priceless to hear her at three years old explain why the animals on Noah's ark did not eat each other: 'They had their seat belts on!'

When she was four and a half a Soviet orchestra came to perform in Los Angeles. We went to protest in front of the concert hall and took Amy along. Numerous Jews were there carrying signs and chanting: 'Let my people go, now!' to ask that their relatives be allowed to leave the Soviet Union. We had mobilised Christian friends to give out pamphlets denouncing the persecution of Christians in Communist countries, and requesting freedom for our imprisoned brethren. Amy was helping too and very successfully: no one refused to take the pamphlets she was handing out with a smile.

That evening she prayed:

> Our Father,
> Let our people go, help them be free
> Help the children in India,
> Give them food, clothing and toys.
> Thank you for life, liberty and justice.
> In Jesus' name, Amen.

At five she told us, 'I know why they called your city Bucharest (pronounced book-arrest): because, if they caught you with a Bible, they would arrest you!'

Spurgeon wrote that when God abolished paradise, he left a corner of it untouched – a true Christian home. I consider it a wife's foremost achievement and a constant source of joy. In this I hope to equal my mother-in-law. Her smile and her deliberate silence, even in the most difficult circumstances, are admirable. She has a saying, 'Even God cannot contradict one who is silent.' This is one reason why her rare speech and her own book (*The Pastor's Wife*, Hodder & Stoughton) are so much appreciated.

Today Pastor and Mrs Wurmbrand still travel around the

world on speaking tours, while Michael, I, and the staff of 'Jesus to the Communist World' press on with our campaign in fifty-three countries. We know that God has chosen to work through men. The Jewish people were slaves in Egypt. It was all God's doing when they escaped, but his tool was Moses.

We, too, are workers together with God. We know of families of Christian martyrs who would have literally died of hunger if our mission had not provided for them. We know of churches which could not have resisted Communist pressure and indoctrination without the Bibles we have smuggled in. While we thank the Lord for blessing our efforts we remember the many dedicated people in our missions, the many contributors and prayer-partners throughout the world who have played their part during the twelve years since our mission began. In gratitude to the Lord and the many who help, I would like to share some of the accomplishments which, however slightly, have improved life for our brethren under the icy grip of Communism.

A chip of the cross

The most obvious, horrifying, and physically constricting grip that Communism has on its people is imprisonment. Thousands of Christians suffer in jails for their religious beliefs.

When a person is imprisoned, the relatives are deprived of earning a living, harassed and despised, so that the prisoner's anguish is increased by knowing that his family suffers too. One Baptist pastor was sentenced to ten years' imprisonment, leaving behind his wife and six small children. We were able to help his family, and received the following letter from his wife:

> God has given me the privilege of bearing a chip of the cross of Christ. My children ask me when Daddy will return, but their father put his life at stake for his faith. When he was arrested the Communists beat us viciously.
> 'You and your children will starve,' they told me. But love has a long arm, and from beyond the ocean we received your help. Now the Communists are put to shame.

We feel such jewels of faith are an unsurpassed reward for our relief work and we gladly share them with the Church at large.

We smuggle money to persecuted dependents – we are talking about children whose only crime is that of having Christian parents.

Failure or success of Christianity in every mission field depends considerably upon the availability of the Scriptures in the appropriate languages. An Ethiopian Christian took the Gospel to heathen Africa in the early days of the Christian faith but after a brief time of flourishing, the message decayed because the Christians themselves did not translate and distribute the Scriptures in the local Amharic dialect. We therefore are engaged in smuggling Bibles and portions of Bibles in dozens of languages to Russia and other Communist countries.

One of Michael's most audacious ideas in this connection was to place a gospel tract inside a polythene cheese-bag (he thought of this while shopping in the supermarket!), enclose a straw inside so that it would float, then vacuum-seal it. We have dropped millions of these by balloons, ships, or planes to the shores of Russia, China, North Korea, Cuba and Albania, wherever our couriers could not go as 'tourists'.

The Soviet Christians have confirmed the arrival of such packages, some of which have even reached inmates in labour-camps. The Soviet government was so incensed that it went to the trouble of making a film against our organisation, besides attacking us by name in several books and innumerable articles.

A Soviet Christian who succeeded in escaping to West Germany recounted in public meetings how he and others had 'fished' along the Baltic seashores for the Christian literature we had launched on the sea currents. The underground churches of the Soviet Union had been told in code, beforehand, approximately when they could expect these packs. Through informers the secret police also got wind of it, and posted their men to wait as well. Nothing happened, so they decided that the information had been false, and left. The literature arrived later: it was as if the waves had waited for the Communists' departure. This brother had transported part of this literature from the Baltic shore all the way across Russia, as far as the Soviet-Chinese frontier.

One of our happiest moments was the day the following letter arrived from deep within Red China.

I got the booklet concerning personal problems. Its name is *The Only Way*. The book was given to me by a comrade. Even now nobody knows who sent it, but most of us understand that God himself did. XY has not returned yet from an indoctrination course (a euphemism for prison in China), but she also received the book. Do you think you can help us some more?

We rejoiced to learn that Christian books had arrived in Red China, and had even reached a Christian jailed there.

Marxism has created a language of its own, and though it has existed for over a hundred years, nobody had yet translated the Scriptures into this new language. We claimed the privilege of doing so. My father-in-law, with his extensive knowledge of both Marxism and the Bible, wrote a book: *Answer to Moscow's Bible* (Hodder and Stoughton) which is actually the Gospel truth explained in Marxist jargon. By now it has been published and distributed in many languages spoken behind the Iron Curtain as well as in the West.

Every year we also broadcast thousands of hours of Christian messages. To Albania and Red China, for instance, we read the Bible at dictation speed. Letters from the mainland confirmed they have been heard and copies were made by the listeners and passed around in deadly secrecy.

We are not the only broadcasters for Communist countries, but, in their publications, the Reds specifically attack our programmes entitled 'The Gospel in Marxist Language', which have converted even Communists. Here is the text of a letter received by our mission as a result of such a broadcast in Latin America:

Peru, 23rd of September, 1974
Dear Sir,
I am writing you this letter from a guerrilla camp in the jungles of my homeland, Peru. It was one in the morning, last February, in the middle of the jungle, as I lay unable to sleep. I was depressed, sad, and for some reason afraid. Afraid of what, I do not know, but I can assure you I had no fear of bullets. So I was searching for some programme on my portable radio to cheer me up. The programmes of

my comrades had become empty to me; they were repetitious and filled with hatred for one's neighbour.

In this state of mind I came across the Voice of Friendship. A programme was just beginning. I listened in silence and with complete attention to a reading of *The Bible in Marxist Language.* The passage was somewhere in St Matthew, I don't remember where exactly, where Jesus, the great teacher, spoke of forgiving one's enemies. That passage drove itself into the deepest part of my being, and lodged there. Suddenly I experienced peace, and it caused me to weep like a child. Even now I don't understand what happened. All I know is that in my heart there was hate. Hate for the rich; hate for those who have treated us unjustly. You see, my parents were the victims of an exploiting land owner. But look! For some reason I don't hate them any more. I can't explain it. Oh, if this heart that beats within this green jacket could be free of its hates, free to love everyone. Is it possible for me?

Believe it or not, that was the only time I heard your programme until the 13th of this month. How happy I have become, Don Ricardo (name used by Pastor Wurmbrand in the broadcast); now I shall not miss a single one of your programmes. Please have the manager send me a schedule. Send me too the booklet *Tortured for Christ* and, if possible, a Bible in Marxist language, the New Testament or part of it anyway. I would thank you very much, and tenderly, because I want to read the Book of Books. Actually, any translation would do. Cordially, . . . (Name and address omitted by translator).

Partly due to public opinion generated by our actions some Christians have been released from Communist jails – Cardinal Sljipy, Bishop Welychkowsky, the brethren Klassen, Hartfeld, Rose and Jundt, to name only a heroic few.

Another Soviet Christian, Eugen Bressenden, whose mother has spent ten years in prison for her faith, (he himself spent three) is now in the United States. He told us how thankful he was to receive four parcels from us after coming out of prison: it had proved to the Communists that he was known abroad. This prevented Bressenden from being placed in a psychiatric asylum as had been previously planned by the Reds.

We have also 'bought out' some prisoners. Among them, we are thankful to say, was Alice, the dear Christian lady who took care of Michael when both his parents were in prison for their faith. She knew she would be made to suffer for this simple act of kindness, and she did. She had to spend five years in prison, her teeth kicked out in beatings and two ribs broken. Communists do claim, after all, that they render equal rights to women.

Recently God enabled our mission to be the first and only one yet to succeed in making a documentary film on life in a Russian concentration camp. The pictures were shot with telephoto equipment. You can see the prisoners and their guards, the big dogs watching them, the installations of the camp. I had the privilege of reading the narration for this film, *Christians behind Bars*. It was shown on major television networks, not only in the United States but all over the world. After seeing it, the Communist Parties of France, Italy and Japan protested to the Soviets about the existence of such concentration camps. As a result new rifts have appeared between Communist groups in the free world.

A good friend of ours, in whose home the foundations of our Norwegian sister mission have been established, became head of an American school in Norway. Some children of Communist diplomats also attend the school. This lady met one man from the Romanian embassy who came to pick up his child. She gave him some of our literature. Reading it, he was deeply affected. Soon afterwards he came to her and confessed he was a spy. His confessions unveiled a whole network of forty Communist spies, who were subsequently imprisoned.

We have also seen the influence of our publications on the elections in different countries such as Chile, Portugal, Sweden, West Germany, Japan and Australia where leftist governments have failed to get the upper hand. We did not participate in any political campaign, but our publications in those countries simply exposed the evils of Communism and warned people of its disastrous effects. Our mission has been the only one daring to oppose the Communists while they still held power in Chile and Portugal. At the peak of Communist terror in Portugal, when the Red elements could bomb and kill unpunished, our local workers dared to publish Christian anti-Communist material.

From many countries where we are active we hear, 'If only you could work more, speak louder and spread your literature wider, we could turn our country around in the right direction.'

Yet our work is not easy. Our trustee in Uganda, and a courier who smuggled literature from Macao into Red China, have both been killed. We are continually attacked by the Communist press of Russia and Eastern Germany. There have been many threats and two actual assaults on the life of my father-in-law. Every now and then I feel the temptation to return to a quiet life. My husband and I could earn a living otherwise, and worship God in stillness, without all the excitement, stress and perils of mission-work. But since we have dedicated ourselves to this, we are going to continue until we receive clear indication from the Lord to change direction.

In our family we often talk about famous missionaries. One who impressed me was Dr Lambie of the Sudan Interior Mission. He worked with one of the most backward tribes, daily enduring danger from scorpions, poisonous snakes and malaria-bearing insects. Then he came on furlough to the United States. Here a good job was offered him and he was inclined to accept it. His conscience was clear; he had had his share of hardships and had stood up to them. But while attending a Christian meeting, he had a vision; he saw a map of Northeastern Africa, from the centre of it a hand was stretched out toward him, pleading, beckoning – a deformed leper's hand. He reluctantly shook it. Then surprise – it was no longer a leper's hand but that of Christ with the imprint of a nail in the palm.

There are many hands stretched out from behind the Iron Curtain. They ask for God's word. I see hands reaching out from behind iron bars asking for a piece of bread for their children. Under these circumstances the time to rest for a Christian is after death. Therefore as a family we shall continue our ministry.

It is said that King David kept in a room of his palace the shepherd coat and staff he had used as a boy. When tempted by pride, he would go to that room and remember that it was God's grace alone which had elevated him. From time to time I also pay a visit to the chamber of past memories, and recall that I was born a slave under the Communists, the daughter of Jews who had suffered terribly, and that I have been raised from the pit of sin by Jesus. Now I am called to make my small contribution to a far-reaching mission. This is God's work, and marvellous in my eyes!

Customers or disciples?

Now, thirteen years after I first recognised Christ as the Messiah, I am glad that I surrendered my heart, mind and life to him as the Master. In his hand I can be the brush which paints a beautiful image which can defy time.

Here in the United States, with all the freedom to work, talk, worship and travel, my time seems to fly and I now regret the wasted years full of fears, uncertainties and misery in our native Communist 'paradise'. But one day the Lord showed me that he is truly Master of everything. I read from the prophet Joel (Joel 2:25, 26),

> And I will restore to you the years that the locust hath eaten . . . And ye shall eat in plenty, and be satisfied, and praise the name of the Lord your God, that hath dealt wondrously with you; and my people shall never be ashamed.

Indeed we experienced that precious promise, and more. Besides freedom he has also given us success in our efforts to serve him by helping his forgotten children in Communist countries.

My father-in-law has divided Christians into two categories: customers of Christ and disciples of Christ. Many people become his customers by accepting salvation; it certainly makes life's puzzles and pressures much easier. I, for one, am a very satisfied customer, and as the years go by I find that Christ really has no competition.

But there is another category, a step higher: when a customer tells Christ, 'It must be wonderful to wipe away tears, to bless children, to enlighten minds with truth and to heal broken hearts, to open the gates of heaven for sinners and to go from place to place, doing good. Please would you teach me also to do this?' Out of love, the customer has decided to help each day by carrying Christ's yoke (Matthew 11:29, 30). Then he or she starts to become a disciple.

Today, the yoke of Christ is carried by every persecuted Christian, ŏur brethren in faith, who are still bearing the sufferings from which our family escaped. The Epistle to the Hebrews urges, 'Remember them who are in bonds, as bound with them' (Hebrews 13:3). As a family we are fully dedicated to this. In helping our brethren carry their cross there is satisfaction, and purpose, and fulfilment.

I pray that you, too, will discover this for yourself.

You may write to
Judy Wurmbrand at:

Christian Mission to the Communist World
P.O. Box 19
Bromley BR1 1DJ
Kent

or

Jesus To The Communist World
P.O. Box 11
Glendale
California 91209
U.S.A.